THE SKELETON AND MUSCLES

Steve Parker

HODDER
Wayland

an imprint of Hodder Children's Books

Titles in the series:
The Brain and Nervous System • Digestion
The Heart, Lungs and Blood • Reproduction
The Senses • The Skeleton and Muscles

For more information on this series and other Hodder Wayland titles, go www.hodderwayland.co.uk

Produced by Monkey Puzzle Media Ltd
Gissing's Farm, Fressingfield, Suffolk IP21 5SH, UK

Text copyright © 2003 Steve Parker
Series copyright © 2003 Hodder Wayland
First published in 2003 by Hodder Wayland
an imprint of Hodder Children's Books
Reprinted in 2003
This paperback edition published in 2006

Commissioning Editor: Victoria Brooker
Book Editor: Nicola Edwards
Design: Jane Hawkins
Picture Research: Sally Cole
Artwork: Alex Pang
Consultant: Dr Trish Groves

British Library Cataloguing in Publication Data
Parker, Steve, 1952-
    The skeleton and muscles. – (Our bodies)
    1. Human skeleton – Juvenile literature
    2. Musculoskeletal system – Juvenile literature
    I.Title
    612.7

ISBN 07502 3720 1

Printed and bound in China

Hodder Children's Books
A division of Hodder Headline Limited
338 Euston Road, London NW1 3BH

Picture Acknowledgements
Alamy 9, 13, 34–35; Corbis 5 (Robbie Jack), 30 (Steve Prezant); Corbis Digital Stock *front cover inset*, 37 right; Digital Vision 1, 23 top, 29, 40; FLPA 35 (Chris Mattison); Getty Images *front cover main image* (Taxi), 33 bottom (Stone), 39 (Taxi), 45 (The Image Bank); ImageState 24, 31, 37 left; Panos 11; Robert Harding Picture Library 7, 23 bottom (Tony Gervis); Science Photo Library 4 (Simon Fraser), 14 (NASA), 15 (Athenais, ISM), 17, 19 bottom (Pr. S Cinti/CNRI), 20 (BSIP Ducloux), 21 (Astrid & Hanns-Frider Michler), 26 (Deep Light Productions), 38 (Salisbury District Hospital), 44 (Princess Margaret Rose Hospital); Wellcome Trust 43.

CONTENTS

INTRODUCTION

Supporting parts

Many parts of the body are soft and flexible – the nerves and brain, heart and blood vessels, stomach and intestines are all squishy and bendy. To stop the body sagging onto the floor like a heap of jelly, it is held up by a very strong set of supporting parts, called bones. Each bone is rigid and strong, and all the bones together form the body's inner framework, which allows us to stand tall and move about.

BETWEEN BONES

Bones are not separate parts, distant from each other and scattered around the body. They are linked together at joints, of many different sizes and designs. Joints hold the bones together so they do not come apart but do let them move in relation to each other. Joints also reduce wear and tear, stopping the ends of the bones rubbing and scraping against each other as they move to and fro.

The body's inner supporting framework, called the skeleton, shows up clearly in this whole-body scan as pale white-mauve bones of many sizes and shapes.

PULLING BONES

Bones cannot move by themselves. They are moved by muscles. The body has hundreds of muscles, ranging from large and powerful ones, like those in the hips and upper legs, to tiny and delicate muscles deep inside the ear. Muscles have one main task: to get shorter, or contract. Most muscles are firmly joined to bones. As a muscle contracts, it pulls on the bones and moves them nearer to each other. This moves body parts, from

Dancers train to ensure their muscles are strong and their joints are flexible or supple, so that they can take up hundreds of different body positions.

a finger or toe to a whole arm or leg, or the neck and back.

The muscles, bones and joints make up the musculo-skeletal system. This system supports us and enables us to move around, jump, run, lift and pull objects. It also allows us to smile, shout, clap and even breathe.

THE SKELETON

In the middle

If you were to take away a body's skin, nerves, blood vessels, muscles, guts and other soft parts, the last items left, in the middle of the body, would be the bones. The adult human body has a total of 206 bones, and together, they are known as the skeleton. Bones make up about one-sixth of the body's total weight.

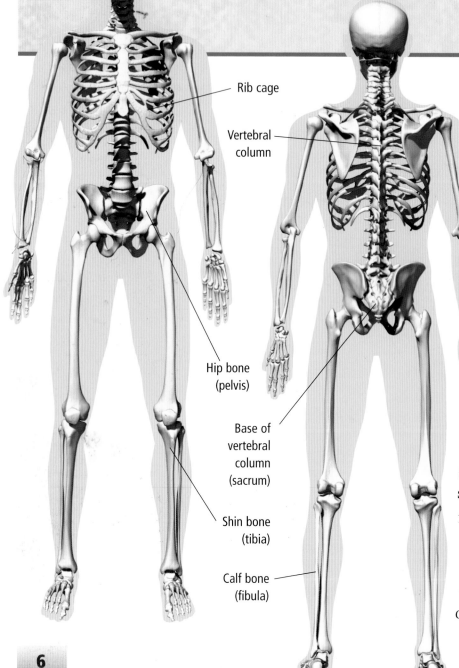

Rib cage

Vertebral column

Hip bone (pelvis)

Base of vertebral column (sacrum)

Shin bone (tibia)

Calf bone (fibula)

Seen from the rear, the skeleton looks different from the front view, especially the skull and vertebral column of backbones.

BUSY BONES

Old bones and skeletons, in museums and exhibitions, usually look dry, dull, whitened, flaking and brittle. But inside the body, living bones are quite different. They are greyish and damp-looking, slightly bendy, and very much alive. Like other body parts, they have blood vessels and nerve connections. They even change shape slowly and

ANIMAL VERSUS HUMAN

Sharks are powerful hunters of the open ocean. Like us, they have a skeleton – yet there is not a single bone in a shark's body. Its skeleton is made entirely of cartilage (gristle) rather than bone.

The shark has ribs and many other skeletal parts – but made of cartilage, not bone.

slightly through life, in response to stresses and strains on the body, and its patterns of movement. This can happen when someone changes from one sport or activity to another, for example, switching from hurdling to horse-riding.

NAMES OF BONES

Every bone has a scientific or medical name. In fact, every part of every bone – each lump or bump, hollow or curve – has its own scientific name. Many bones also have more ordinary, everyday names. Examples are the kneecap, which is known scientifically

as the patella, and the cheek bone, called the zygomatic bone. The 'funny bone' is not a whole bone; rather it is formed by the elbow ends of the long bones called the humerus in the upper arm, and the ulna in the forearm.

CARTILAGE

Bone is the skeleton's main structural substance, and it is very strong. But the body has another structural substance called cartilage or 'gristle'. Cartilage is similar in many ways to bone, but it is slightly softer and bendier. With bone, it forms parts of the skeleton, especially in the ribs in the chest. Cartilage also covers the ends of bones in joints and makes up several structural parts of the body, such as the nose and ears.

weblinks

To find out more about the skeleton, go to:
www.waylinks.co.uk/series/ourbodies/skelandmus

Try this!

If you press your nose and tweak your ear, they bend. They have cartilage inside, to support them and give them shape. If they were bone, they would be very stiff indeed. Knocked hard, they might snap off!

Layer upon layer

A bone is like a piece of wood – light, tough, hard, strong, and slightly bendy. But, unlike wood, bone is not the same all the way through. Most bones have three layers, one inside the other.

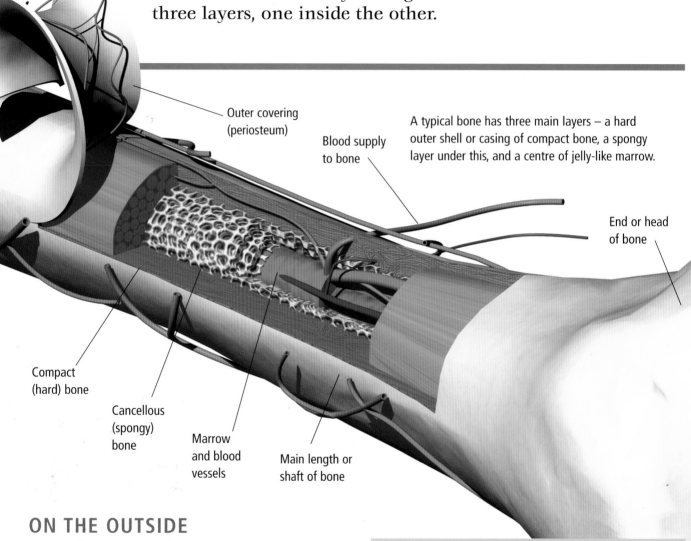

Outer covering (periosteum)

Blood supply to bone

A typical bone has three main layers – a hard outer shell or casing of compact bone, a spongy layer under this, and a centre of jelly-like marrow.

End or head of bone

Compact (hard) bone

Cancellous (spongy) bone

Marrow and blood vessels

Main length or shaft of bone

ON THE OUTSIDE

The outer layer is known as compact or hard bone. It provides most of the toughness and strength. Compact bone is made of thousands of tiny rod-shaped parts called osteons, packed together like drinking straws in a box. Each osteon is thinner than a human hair and consists of layers of hard mineral crystals.

MICRO-BODY

In each osteon, crystals and fibres are arranged in wider and wider layers, like smaller tubes inside larger tubes. In the hole along the middle are microscopic blood vessels and a tiny nerve.

The crystals, mainly calcium, phosphate and carbonate, are scattered among bundles of thread-like fibres of another substance, the protein collagen.

IN THE MIDDLE

Inside compact bone is a layer of cancellous or spongy bone. It is a mass of collagen fibres and mineral crystals, like compact bone, but it also contains thousands of small, bubble-like holes. Cancellous bone is quite strong, and also very light. It helps to reduce the weight of the whole bone and allows it to be slightly flexible, so that under great stress, it is more likely to bend rather than snap.

ON THE INSIDE

Most bones have a soft, jelly-like centre, called bone marrow. This is very active, making microscopic new red and white blood cells for the whole body's blood system, to replace blood cells which naturally wear out and die. Bone marrow is very busy. Every second, the marrow in the body's bones makes two million new red cells, and tens of thousands of new white cells.

ANIMAL VERSUS HUMAN

We have our bones on the inside. Some animals have bone on the outside too. Tortoises, armadillos and pangolins have body coverings made of bony plates, for protection. The bone is covered by another tough substance, horn.

The giant tortoise's shell has bony plates covered by plates of tough, hard horn.

THE GROWING SKELETON

THE UNBORN BABY

Like other body parts, the bones of an unborn baby start to develop when it is tiny, hardly larger than your thumb. But at this very early stage, the 'bones' are not actually made of bone. Their shapes form first as softer, bendier cartilage. Over months in the womb, and then in the years following birth, this cartilage gradually develops mineral crystals and hardens into true bone. This process is called ossification.

STAGES OF GROWTH

The skeleton begins to appear in the form of cartilage, by about the third week after a human body starts to

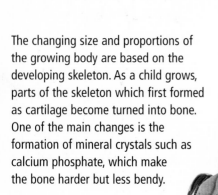

The changing size and proportions of the growing body are based on the developing skeleton. As a child grows, parts of the skeleton which first formed as cartilage become turned into bone. One of the main changes is the formation of mineral crystals such as calcium phosphate, which make the bone harder but less bendy.

develop from the tiny fertilized egg inside its mother's womb. After another five weeks (which is still seven months before birth), some of this cartilage starts to harden into true bone, as the skeleton itself continues to grow in size. This process happens at different rates in different areas of the body. When a baby is born, its skull and backbone are quite well formed and hardened into bone, although they are still growing. The wrist and ankle 'bones' have much less bone – they are still mainly cartilage. The long bones in the arms and legs will not be completely bone until 15-18 years of age, when the person reaches full adult height.

BONE PROBLEMS

Bones need minerals and other substances to become tough and hard. One important substance is vitamin D. If this is lacking in a person's diet, the bone cannot harden fully. It may stay soft and grow in the wrong shape. If this happens during childhood, as the skeleton is growing, it is known as rickets. It can cause problems such as bent or 'bowed' legs. The same problem in adults is known as osteomalacia.

Lack of healthy food makes the bones weak, so they cannot support the body and do not grow in the usual shape.

ANIMAL VERSUS HUMAN

Some animal skeletons develop very fast. A mouse's is fully grown by four weeks! Other animal skeletons never stop developing. A tortoise or crocodile may still be growing at 80 years old – although more slowly than when it was younger.

BONES OF THE SKULL AND FACE

Protection

The main bones inside the head are called the skull and lower jaw. The complicated shape of the skull protects five of the body's most delicate parts – the eyes, ears and brain. The two eyes are set in deep bowls called orbits, in the front of the skull. The tiny inner parts of each ear are inside a chamber within the thickness of the side of the skull, in the temporal bone. And the brain is protected by the curved dome over the top, known as the cranium.

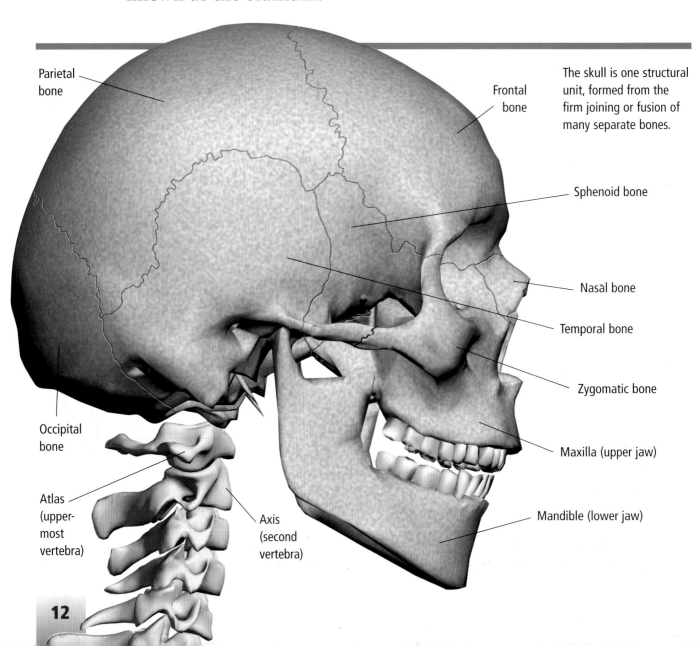

Parietal bone

Frontal bone

The skull is one structural unit, formed from the firm joining or fusion of many separate bones.

Sphenoid bone

Nasal bone

Temporal bone

Zygomatic bone

Occipital bone

Maxilla (upper jaw)

Atlas (upper-most vertebra)

Axis (second vertebra)

Mandible (lower jaw)

The proportions of the skull bone determine the overall shape of the face, from wide to narrow.

THE SMALLEST BONES

The human skull is made of 21 bones linked firmly at suture joints (see page 32). There are seven other bones in the head, too. Six of the bones (three deep inside each ear) are the smallest bones of the entire body. They are called the hammer, anvil and stirrup: the stirrup is hardly larger than this letter U. These bones help us to hear, passing sound vibrations from the eardrum to the innermost ear. The seventh bone is one of the body's strongest – the lower jaw, or mandible. It is moved by muscles that are, for their relative size, some of the body's most powerful. They are the temporalis in front of the ear, and the masseter under the cheek bone. These are the muscles we use to bite and chew.

Top Tips

In risky sports and activities, a helmet or hard-hat or head-guard protects not only your skull, but your eyes and ears – and your brain! In some high-speed activities, like skiing and cycling, you cannot take part unless you are wearing some form of protection for your head.

Try this!

Speak loudly as normal, then hold your nose and speak again. Your voice sounds different. Normally, sounds pass through the nose, and this is linked to air chambers called sinuses, inside the bones of your face. The sounds fill these air chambers and make your voice louder and clearer. If you hold your nose, air cannot pass this way.

HEALTHY BONES

Keeping fit

The body stays fitter, healthier and in better shape, if it keeps active. This is true of all body parts, including bones. Every day, we can make sure that our bones and other body parts have the best chance of staying strong and healthy.

EATING AND BONES

Bones contain minerals such as calcium and phosphate. To keep our bones healthy, we need to eat plenty of these minerals, in a range of foods such as milk, dairy products, meat, fish and fresh fruits and vegetables. In an emergency, when food is lacking, the body can take some of the minerals out of the bones, for more urgent needs elsewhere. But this weakens the bones, and the minerals need to be replaced quickly.

ACTIVITY AND BONES

If muscles are not used regularly, they become weak and gradually waste away. The same happens to bones. They are designed to cope with a certain amount of stress and strain during movement. Most kinds of activity keep bones strong and tough, as well as benefiting other body parts, like the heart and lungs.

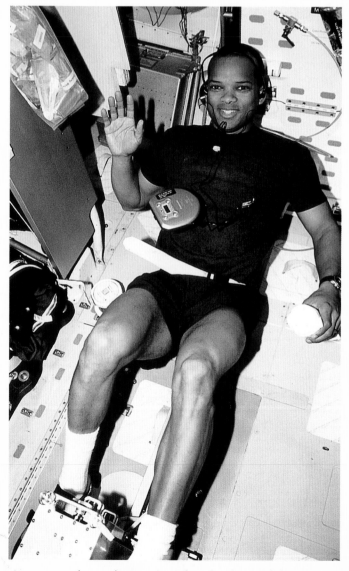

Astronauts take regular exercise, otherwise the weightless conditions of space would weaken their bones and muscles.

Activities range from energetic sports such as football and tennis, to swimming, jogging and even brisk walking. Doing the opposite – sitting and lying down for long periods of time – means that bones lose their strength, and become at greater risk from breaks or other injuries.

HELPING BONES

Bones are tough, but sometimes they are put under so much strain that they crack or even break. This usually happens when the body is moving fast and then stops suddenly – such as in a road accident, a fall or a collision in high-speed sport. So it's important to wear protective clothing and equipment. A helmet protects the skull in the head. Shoulder pads cover the collar bones. Elbow and knee guards protect the bone ends and joints there. In football, shin pads cover the front of the lower leg, which is at risk from the accidental kicks of other players.

This X-ray shows a break (see upper left) in the fibula or calf bone, in the lower leg just above the ankle.

weblinks
To find out more about healthy bones, go to:
www.waylinks.co.uk/series/ourbodies/skelandmus

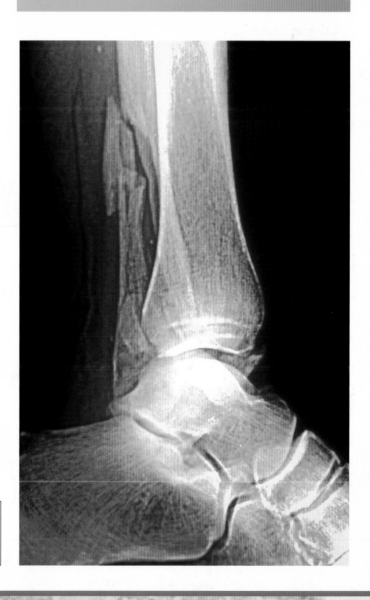

Try this!

Feel where bones are near the surface of the body. They form hard bumps just under the skin. Bones in these places are at risk of cracks or breaks when knocked hard, because they are not covered by softer parts like muscles or fat, which absorb the blow. Examples include the shin, ankle, elbow and collar area.

THE MUSCLE SYSTEM

Making movements

Muscles do almost nothing except become shorter, or contract, and then relax and become longer again. By doing this, they make every movement of the body. This includes not only the movements we see on the outside, such as walking, running and jumping. It also includes movements inside the body, like swallowing, breathing and pumping blood.

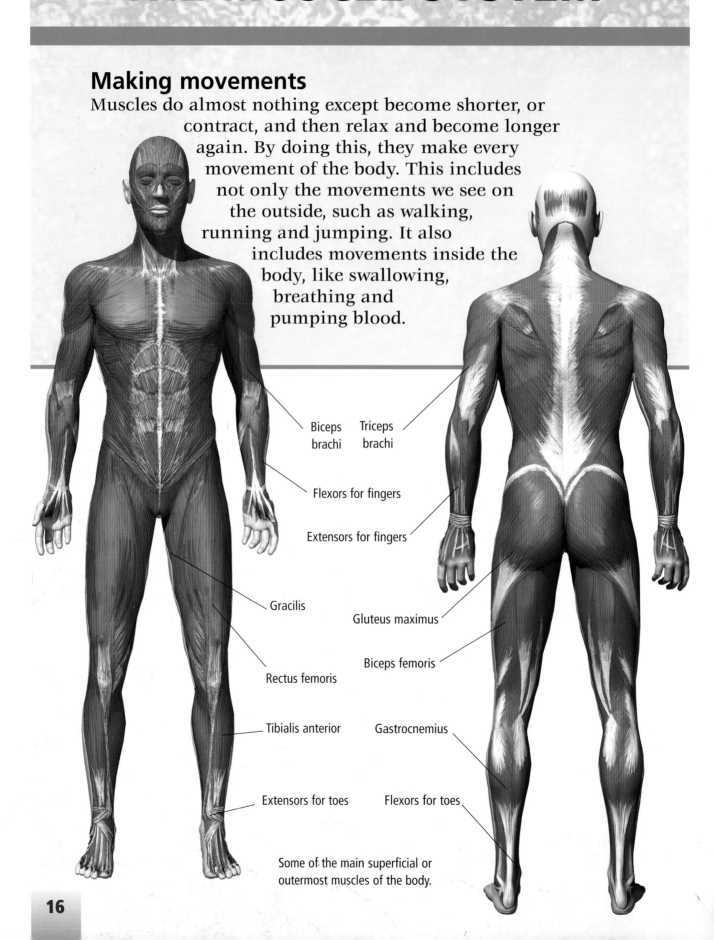

Biceps brachi

Triceps brachi

Flexors for fingers

Extensors for fingers

Gracilis

Gluteus maximus

Rectus femoris

Biceps femoris

Tibialis anterior

Gastrocnemius

Extensors for toes

Flexors for toes

Some of the main superficial or outermost muscles of the body.

MUSCLES AND BONES

The body has about 640 skeletal muscles. These are the muscles which are mainly joined to the bones of the skeleton. Skeletal muscles pull bones to move the body about. Skeletal muscles are also called voluntary muscles, because we can control them in a voluntary way, or at will, by thoughts and decisions. And they are known as striped muscles, because under the microscope, they have a pattern of tiny light and dark stripes. Other kinds of muscle, which are not voluntary and not striped, are shown on the next pages.

MICRO-BODY

Skeletal or striped muscle shows its dark and light bands, or striations, under the microscope. As it gets shorter, the lighter bands become narrower.

The striations (stripes) of skeletal muscle are formed by the overlapping of long, thin substances within them, especially actin and myosin.

Try this!

Instead of bones, wide sheets of muscles protect the front of the abdomen (belly or tummy). Tense and pull them in, as if getting ready to blow out hard. Feel how they form a stiff, strong layer to protect the soft inner parts behind them.

NAMES AND SHAPES

We often think of a muscle as long, bulging in the middle, and thinner at each end where it attaches to a bone. This is true for many muscles in the arms and legs. But there are plenty of other shapes and designs of muscles. Sometimes a muscle's name is taken from its shape or its connections with bones. The deltoid muscle in the shoulder has three sides, like a triangle ('delta' means triangle-shaped). The triceps muscle in the arm is named because it is Y-shaped with three ends, which are called 'heads' in muscles ('tri' means 3, 'ceph' means head).

Different types

Most of the muscles in the body are skeletal muscles (see previous page). They form about two-fifths of the body's whole weight. They pull on bones and move the body about, and we can control them at will. But the body has two other kinds of muscle, known as visceral and cardiac muscle.

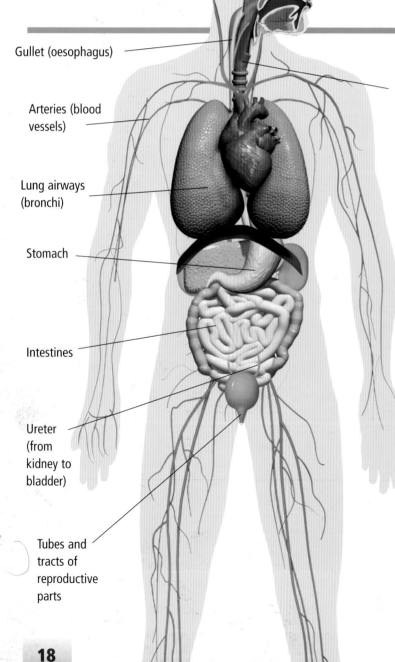

Gullet (oesophagus)

Windpipe (trachea)

Arteries (blood vessels)

Lung airways (bronchi)

Stomach

Intestines

Ureter (from kidney to bladder)

Tubes and tracts of reproductive parts

MUSCLES FOR THE INSIDES

Visceral muscle is found mainly as layers in the walls or coverings of inner body parts like the stomach and intestines, blood vessels, and air tubes in the lungs. It also forms bag-like containers, such as in the bladder. Visceral muscle is sometimes called smooth muscle because, under the microscope, it does not have tiny stripes like skeletal muscle. It looks smooth and flat. Visceral muscle is also known as involuntary muscle. This is because its works automatically, on its own, and we cannot affect it at will, by thinking.

Smooth (visceral or involuntary) muscle is found in many body parts, including the walls of blood vessels that branch throughout the body.

Visceral muscles are not joined to bones. They work by contracting in a wave-like fashion along their length. In a tube, this pushes the contents along. An example is in the intestine (gut), where food is pushed and squeezed along as it is digested. The wave-like squeezing motion is known as peristalsis.

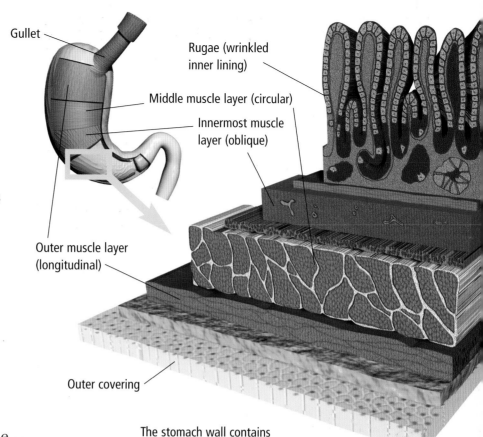

Gullet

Rugae (wrinkled inner lining)

Middle muscle layer (circular)

Innermost muscle layer (oblique)

Outer muscle layer (longitudinal)

Outer covering

The stomach wall contains several layers of smooth muscle, with their fibres arranged in different directions, to allow a wide range of squeezing movements.

HEART MUSCLE

The heart is almost all muscle – a special type called cardiac muscle or myocardium. Skeletal muscles get tired or fatigued if we use them too much. Heart muscle never fatigues – which is fortunate, because it has to contract and pump blood every second, to keep the body alive.

weblinks

To find out more about the smooth muscles, go to:
www.waylinks.co.uk/series/ourbodies/skelandmus

Try this!

Swallow hard while touching your neck to feel the muscles of your gullet (oesophagus), inside your neck. They contract or squeeze like a wave, to push swallowed items down into your stomach.

MICRO-BODY

Under a microscope, visceral muscle lacks the thin stripes or bands of skeletal muscle. Also it can contract for longer periods than skeletal muscle, without getting tired.

Smooth or visceral muscle, magnified 3760 times

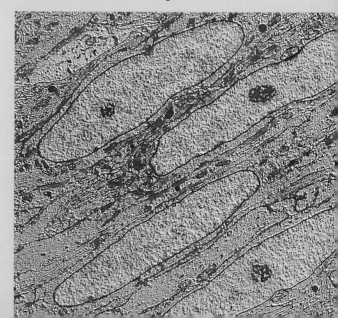

TENDONS

Anchored onto bones

A bulging muscle does not usually join directly to a bone. In most cases, the muscle end tapers into a tough, rope-like, narrower tendon. This is the part which is firmly stuck or anchored onto the bone. Tendons are pale because they have much less blood in them than muscles. They are made mainly of string-like fibres of the body substance collagen (which is also found in bones and in the skin).

LIVING GLUE

At the muscle end, the tendon is joined mainly to the outer layer or 'skin' around the muscle, known as the epimysium. At the bone end, it is joined to a similar outer 'skin' around the bone, called the periosteum. Both of these joins are very strong. It takes great force to pull a tendon from its bone or muscle, or to stretch it so that it tears. If this happens, we often call it a 'strained muscle' or 'torn muscle' when, in fact, it's really the tendon which is injured.

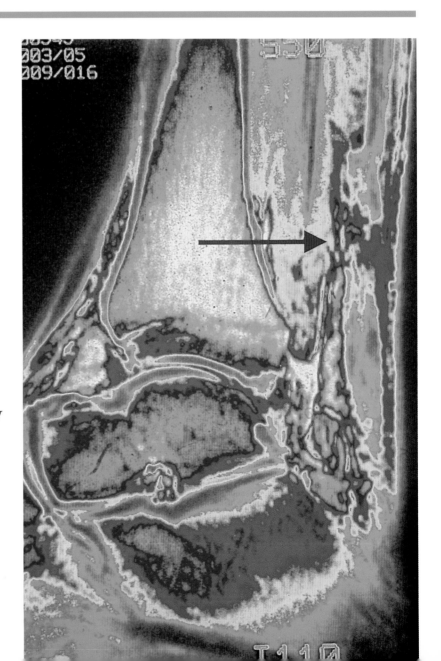

This computer-coloured scan shows an achilles tendon above the heel which was put under excessive strain, resulting in a tear (arrowed).

LONG TENDONS

Some muscles have more than one 'end'. When you curl up your toes, you use a muscle in the front of the lower leg, called an extensor. It has one tendon at its upper end. But at the lower end it branches into three parts, each with a tendon. The three tendons run down through the ankle, and along the top of the foot, to pull on the tops of the toes and make them curl up.

Tendons are pale in colour, partly because they contain little blood compared to well-supplied, blood-rich body parts such as muscles.

Try this!

Stand up straight, then bend your knees to crouch slightly. Feel two large tendons just above the back of your knee, called hamstring tendons, take the strain. Also feel the body's largest tendon, just above the heel, called the calcaneal or achilles tendon.

MICRO-BODY

This microscope view of a tendon shows its strong, stringy fibres, with few blood vessels or nerves. The small blood supply means an injured tendon usually takes a long time to heal.

Muscle fibres

A big muscle contains thousands of long, thin parts called muscle fibres (myofibres). Each one of these is thinner than a human hair. In most muscles the fibres are about three or four centimetres in length, but in a long muscle, they may be 30 centimetres long. The muscle fibres are wrapped in bundles known as fascicles, and the whole muscle is wrapped in a strong outer layer or 'skin' called the epimysium (see page 20).

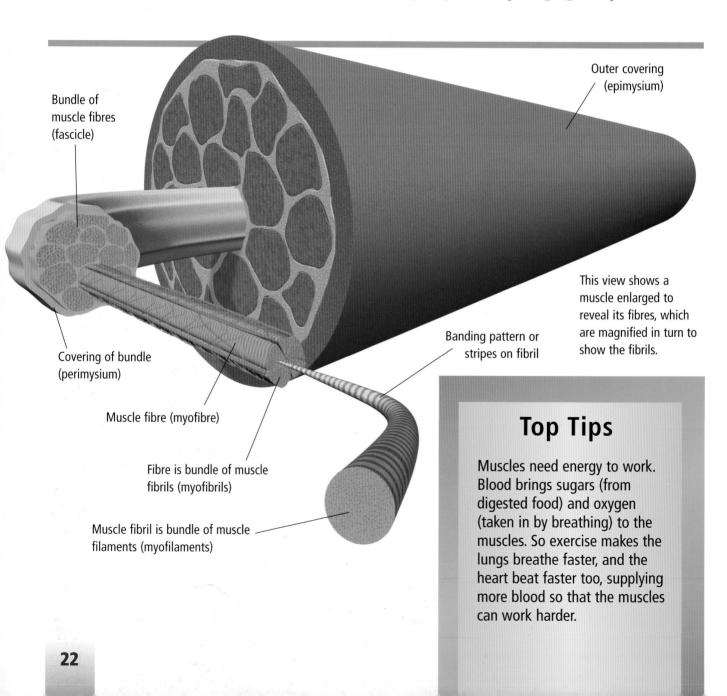

Outer covering (epimysium)

Bundle of muscle fibres (fascicle)

Covering of bundle (perimysium)

Muscle fibre (myofibre)

Fibre is bundle of muscle fibrils (myofibrils)

Muscle fibril is bundle of muscle filaments (myofilaments)

Banding pattern or stripes on fibril

This view shows a muscle enlarged to reveal its fibres, which are magnified in turn to show the fibrils.

Top Tips

Muscles need energy to work. Blood brings sugars (from digested food) and oxygen (taken in by breathing) to the muscles. So exercise makes the lungs breathe faster, and the heart beat faster too, supplying more blood so that the muscles can work harder.

PARTS THAT PULL

A single muscle fibre contains a bundle of even thinner parts, known as muscle fibrils (myofibrils). These have light and dark patches that line up across many fibrils, to give a striped or banded appearance (see page 17). The fibrils are made of two body substances, or proteins, known as actin and myosin. These are long and thin and lie alongside each other, partly overlapping. To make the muscle pull, the actins and myosins slide past each other, so the whole fibril becomes shorter. Most muscles can contract to about two-thirds their length, bulging fatter as they do so.

---
weblinks
To find out more about muscle fibres, go to:
www.waylinks.co.uk/series/ourbodies/skelandmus

In a muscle fibril, actins and myosins move past each other, like people pulling hand-over-hand on a rope.

An adult male gorilla is over one-half muscle.

ANIMAL VERSUS HUMAN

Some animals have far more muscle in their bodies, for their size, than we do. The gorilla is especially strong. It does not have extra muscles compared to us, but each muscle is bigger than the same muscle in a person.

MAKING MOVEMENTS

WORKING TOGETHER

Very few movements in the body use just one muscle. If you bend your elbow, the main muscle involved is the biceps. You can see it bulging in the top of your upper arm. But under this are two more muscles, the coraco-brachialis near the shoulder, and the brachialis lower down towards the elbow. These two help the biceps. At the same time other muscles become tense all down your arm, from shoulder to wrist. Otherwise your shoulder would tilt forwards, and your wrist and hand would go floppy. The 'simple' movement of bending your elbow involves at least 20 muscles!

Hundreds of muscles all over the body are used when dancing to produce graceful, delicately controlled motions.

Try this!

Whirl your arm around at the shoulder like a windmill, and feel the wide range of movements at this joint. It involves at least 50 muscles, which pull or steady the arm in different ways as it goes around in a circle.

24

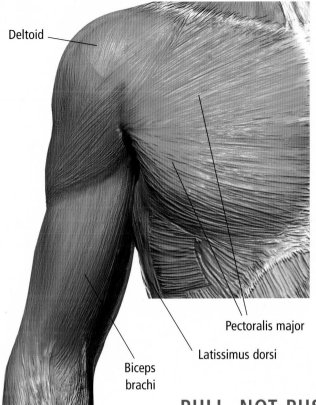

Deltoid

Pectoralis major

Latissimus dorsi

Biceps
brachi

Top Tips

Muscles help to control the amount of movement in a joint, so the bones do not go too far and come apart. Joints should never be forced so that they become painful – pain warns of damage. However gentle bending and flexing, gradually over a long period, helps joints to move farther and more easily.

The shoulder is surrounded and stabilized by many muscles, which move the upper arm and also the elbow.

PULL, NOT PUSH

To straighten your elbow, you do not use the biceps again. A muscle can only pull. It cannot forcefully push to move bones farther apart. The elbow is straightened by the triceps muscle in the underside of your upper arm. As the triceps shortens, the biceps becomes relaxed or floppy, and the movement stretches it longer. So the biceps moves the elbow one way, and the triceps moves it back again. These two muscles are called opposing or antagonistic partners. Straightening the elbow, like bending it, uses a host of other muscles from the shoulder down to the wrist. Nearly all body movements are like this. They use teams of muscles, rather than just one or two.

Twin heads (upper ends) of biceps brachi

Biceps brachi

Triceps brachi

The triceps and biceps are opposing muscle partners. The biceps is so called because it has two ends, or heads, while the triceps has three.

25

CONTROLLING MUSCLES

Nerve messages

Skeletal or voluntary muscles do not move on their own. Otherwise our body actions would be very random, jerky and clumsy! They are controlled by the brain. It sends out messages along nerves, which are like bendy wires that branch throughout the body. Nerve messages are tiny pulses of electricity. The nerve end passes the messages into the muscle fibres, to make these contract. Nerve messages travel very fast, at 100 metres per second or more. So a message's journey, from brain to muscle, takes a fraction of a second.

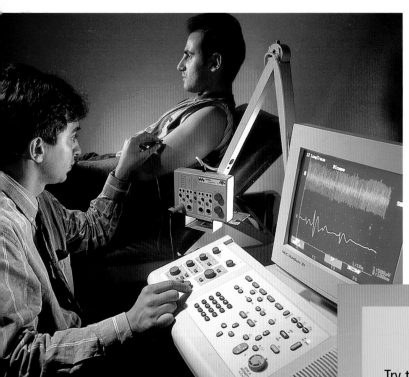

The tiny electrical signals made by active muscles are displayed by an electromyograph (EMG) machine.

MOVEMENTS AND THE BRAIN

The nerve messages to muscles come from several parts of the brain. The main one is the movement centre or motor cortex. This is a strip on the outside of the brain, from the top of the head, down towards the ear. It's the place where we think about, and decide to make or stop, voluntary movements.

Try this!

Try to pat your head with one hand, and rub circles on your stomach with the other, at the same time. It's quite difficult at first because it is an unnatural movement that we rarely do. But keep practising. The brain gradually learns to move the muscles in the right way.

Premotor cortex

Main part of brain (cerebrum)

After leaving the motor cortex, the nerve messages pass through another part of the brain, before they leave along nerves. This is the small, wrinkled cerebellum, at the brain's lower rear.

The cerebellum 'fills in the details' of exactly which muscles should contract, and when, and by how much. We are not usually aware of this. We decide in the motor cortex to make a movement, then go on to other thoughts. The cerebellum takes care of the details. It makes our movements smooth, practised and coordinated – until we have to learn new ones, like playing a piano, rollerblading or windsurfing.

Motor cortex

Cerebellum

Spinal cord

Motor nerve

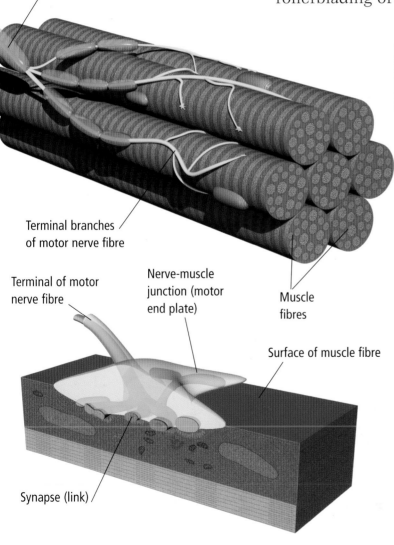

Terminal branches of motor nerve fibre

Terminal of motor nerve fibre

Nerve-muscle junction (motor end plate)

Muscle fibres

Surface of muscle fibre

Synapse (link)

weblinks
To find out more about controlling muscles, go to:
www.waylinks.co.uk/series/ourbodies/skelandmus

Nerve messages from parts of the brain (top) travel along nerves to muscles (left), where the nerve endings are embedded in the hair-fine muscle fibres (bottom).

MICRO-BODY

The motor end plate is a spider-like, microscopic part that joins a nerve end to a muscle. It passes the nerve messages into the muscle fibres, to make them contract.

MUSCLES OF THE FACE AND HEAD

Unusual and useful

Under the skin of the face, there are about 50 muscles. They are among the most unusual and useful in the body. They are unusual because some of them are not joined to bones at each end. They are joined to each other, by straps of fibres. They form a complex web or network of muscles, which can move in hundreds of different ways. These muscles give us a vast range of facial expressions, so we can communicate our thoughts and feelings to other people, without a sound.

Try this!

Make various faces in a mirror, to see how your facial muscles work. Pull your mouth very wide, using the risorius muscle in each cheek. Then curl the corners of your mouth up for a smile, out wider for a grin, and down for a nervous frown.

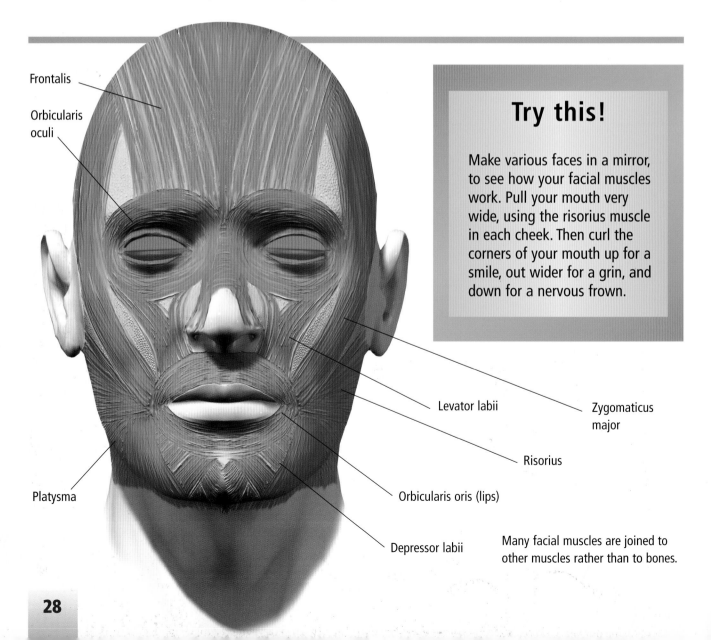

Frontalis

Orbicularis oculi

Platysma

Levator labii

Zygomaticus major

Risorius

Orbicularis oris (lips)

Depressor labii

Many facial muscles are joined to other muscles rather than to bones.

OPEN AND SHUT

Each eyelid is a four-part, circle-shaped muscle called the orbicularis oculi. It has a large opening in the middle – which we see through! When this muscle contracts, the upper and lower parts come together, to close the opening. This is how we blink our eyelids and shut our eyes. There is a similar but larger circle-like muscle in the lips, the orbicularis oris. When it contracts, the mouth closes.

BENDIEST MUSCLE

The body's most bendy muscle is just behind the lips. It's the tongue. In fact a tongue has 12 separate muscles. It is much longer in total, than the part you can see. It is anchored at its lower end, down in the throat and neck region. The tongue can twist and curve into many shapes, from short and wide to long and thin. Using the tongue we can eat, lick, swallow, suck, speak, and even whistle.

ANIMAL VERSUS HUMAN

Lizards do not seem to laugh or frown. In fact, they cannot, even if they wanted. They have fewer and less complicated muscles in their faces. Only a few animals can make lots of facial expressions, mainly monkeys and apes.

weblinks
To find out more about the muscles of the face and head, go to: www.waylinks.co.uk/series/ourbodies/skelandmus

The chimp's lips are very flexible, able to make many facial expressions as well as to gather small food items.

BONE AND MUSCLE DISORDERS

Injuries

Bones and muscles are the body's most physical parts, carrying out endless movements, often under stress and strain. Sometimes the stress becomes too much, and something 'snaps'.

A fracture is a crack, split or complete break in a bone. As a bone heals after a break or fracture, microscopic cells in the bone form new fibres and mineral crystals. After a few months, the break is hardly visible. A dislocation is where two bones in a joint, which are supposed to be held next to each other, come away from each other. A sprained joint is when the bones move farther than they should in relation to each other, stretching or tearing the parts around, like muscles and ligaments. (see page 33.)

TREATMENT

The usual treatment for these injuries is for a doctor to check that all parts are back in their correct places, with an operation if necessary. This is followed by resting the affected part, then very gradual movements and gentle exercises.

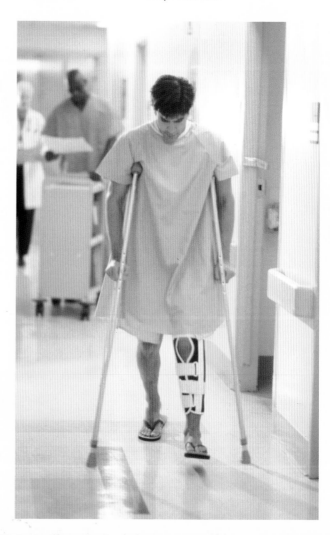

Crutches help to take the weight off an injured leg while it is exercised to keep it mobile.

WASTED MUSCLES

Compared to most other body parts, muscles do not suffer from many diseases. In paralysis, a body part cannot be moved. This is more often due to a problem in the brain or nerves that control a muscle, rather than in the muscle itself. In muscular dystrophy, the muscle fibres do not work properly because of a problem in the way they use the mineral calcium, which helps to control their contraction. The muscles become weak and wasted.

WEAK BONES

Because bones are the body's support system, any problem which reduces their strength can have widespread effects. In osteoporosis, bones lose their hard mineral structure and become weak, brittle and crumbly. This condition tends to affect older women because their bodies have stopped producing certain natural body chemicals, or hormones, which help to keep bones strong. Osteoporosis is also made more likely by smoking, unhealthy eating with not enough vitamins and minerals, and lack of exercise. It can often be treated by tablets, and by gradual activity to strengthen the bones again.

weblinks

To find out more about bone and muscle disorders, go to:
www.waylinks.co.uk/series/ourbodies/skelandmus

Top Tips

In some sports and activities, special joint supports or strappings are recommended. These give extra support to certain joints which are at risk of coming apart or dislocating, due to the patterns of movement involved in the sport. Examples of supports include bandages, strappings or lightweight plastic shields on the shoulders, elbows, wrists, knees and ankles.

Warm-up exercises show if any strapping or support is needed.

Where bones meet

A joint is a structure where two bones meet. Not all joints are flexible, allowing the bones to move in relation to each other. In some parts, such as the skull, the individual bones are firmly linked, as if glued together. In other parts, such as the arms and legs, there are synovial joints which allow various amounts and directions of movements.

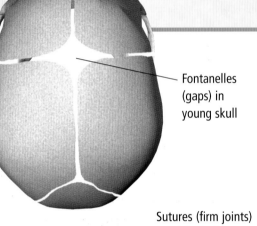

Fontanelles (gaps) in young skull

Sutures (firm joints) in adult skull

The bones of a baby's skull (top) gradually grow together at suture joints during childhood (above).

FIXED JOINTS

The skull seems like one bone, but it is really made up of 21 bones, fixed to each other by rigid joins called suture joints. In a suture joint, tough fibres grow between the bones, along their edges, then gradually shrink to pull the bones closer together. The fibres also become hardened by minerals, almost like real bone. This whole process takes a year or two. A newborn baby's skull bones have not quite locked solid, and there are gaps between, called fontanelles, which the bones grow into and fill. This structure allows the baby's head to squeeze slightly smaller as it emerges from the womb along the narrow birth canal.

FLEXIBLE JOINTS

In a synovial joint, such as the shoulder, the ends of the bones are covered with smooth, shiny, slightly soft cartilage. This allows the bones to slide past each other without wear. A tough synovial capsule surrounds the joint like a bag. Its lining makes slippery synovial fluid.

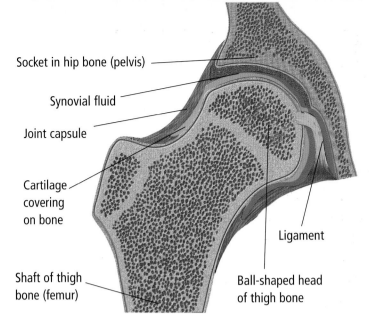

Socket in hip bone (pelvis)

Synovial fluid

Joint capsule

Cartilage covering on bone

Shaft of thigh bone (femur)

Ligament

Ball-shaped head of thigh bone

These views show the inside of the hip joint (left) and the ligaments and other coverings (below).

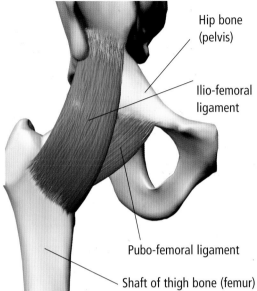

Hip bone (pelvis)

Ilio-femoral ligament

Pubo-femoral ligament

Shaft of thigh bone (femur)

Synovial fluid works like lubricating oil in a car's engine, so that the joint can move smoothly without rubbing or friction.

LIGAMENTS

In a flexible joint, such as the knee, the bones are held near each other by strong, slightly elastic, strap-shaped parts called ligaments. Each ligament is anchored at one end to one bone, and at the other end, to the other bone. In most joints there are several ligaments spaced out around the joint. Ligaments are strong, but they may sprain or tear under sudden strain.

Top Tips

Do warm-up exercises for muscles and joints before strenuous exercise.

Wear suitable protection to avoid excessive flexing or twisting of joints.

Treat a sprain with rest, and use an ice pack to reduce swelling.

If there is no improvement within 36–48 hours, or if the pain and stiffness are severe or worsen, always consult a doctor.

Elbow and knee pads protect these joints from hard knocks and falls.

KEEPING JOINTS HEALTHY

ALLOWING MOVEMENT

Each joint's design allows a certain range of movement. The ball-and-socket design, such as the hip or shoulder, permits great flexibility but little twisting (rotation of the bone). In the back, each gliding-pivot joint includes a pad of cartilage, the intervertebral disc, which is like a cushion between the individual backbones (vertebrae). The joint can flex and twist only slightly, but over the whole backbone this adds up to considerable movement.

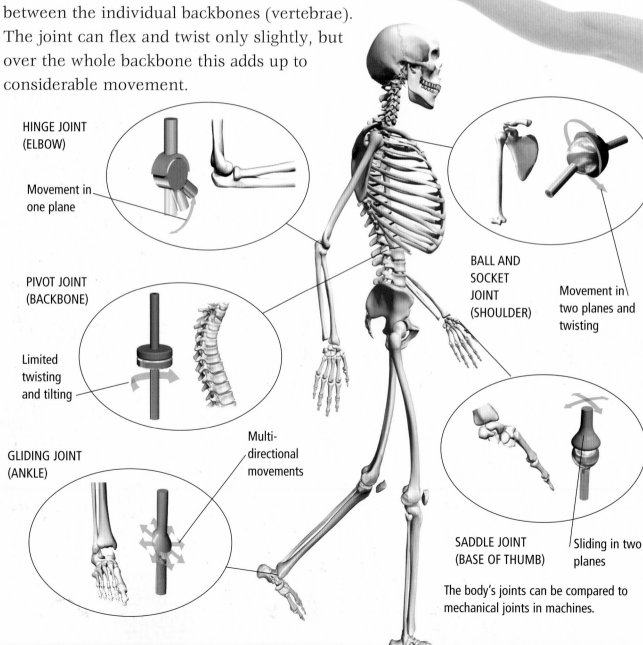

HINGE JOINT (ELBOW)

Movement in one plane

PIVOT JOINT (BACKBONE)

Limited twisting and tilting

GLIDING JOINT (ANKLE)

Multi-directional movements

BALL AND SOCKET JOINT (SHOULDER)

Movement in two planes and twisting

SADDLE JOINT (BASE OF THUMB)

Sliding in two planes

The body's joints can be compared to mechanical joints in machines.

HEALTHY JOINTS

The joints of a young person are more flexible than those of an older person. But old age does not always mean stiff, aching joints. Varied activities and exercises – especially those which are physically not too stressful, like brisk walking, swimming and yoga – can keep the joints healthy and supple for many years. Sudden twists and turns, where great strain is put on joints, should generally be avoided.

Gymnasts follow special training routines to keep their muscles strong and joints supple.

ANIMAL VERSUS HUMAN

Some snakes have more than 200 vertebrae, or individual backbones. So they are very flexible and bendy, compared to a human, with 26 backbones. Some animals have far fewer vertebrae – most frogs have only eight.

A snake's backbone can coil around many times.

HOW THE HAND WORKS

Amazing tools

Our hands and fingers are amazing tools. They can grip and squeeze tightly, spread out wide to rub and stroke, and make the tiniest movements to pick up a pin. This is made possible by their many small bones, joints and muscles. The wrist has eight bones, known as carpals. The palm has five, called metacarpals. And there are three small bones in each finger and two in the thumb, all known as phalanges.

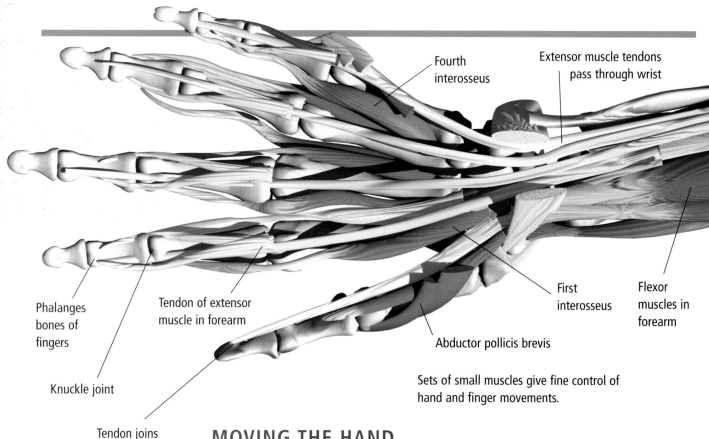

Fourth interosseus

Extensor muscle tendons pass through wrist

Phalanges bones of fingers

Knuckle joint

Tendon of extensor muscle in forearm

Tendon joins to thump tip

Abductor pollicis brevis

First interosseus

Flexor muscles in forearm

Sets of small muscles give fine control of hand and finger movements.

MOVING THE HAND

Each hand contains about 15 small muscles that move the thumb and fingers at their joints, called knuckles. In particular, they waggle the fingers from side to side at their knuckle joints with the palm. There are also six large muscles in the forearm which move the fingers. They have very long tendons that pass through the wrist and join to the fingers along their length. These mainly bend and straighten the fingers.

PRECISION AND POWER

The human hand is so useful, partly because it has a thumb. This can 'oppose' the fingers, when the tip of the thumb touches the tip of each finger in turn. No animal can do this. It gives us the precision grip to pick up something as small as a grain of rice very delicately, using the thumb and any other finger. It can also create the power grip, where the thumb and fingers wrap around each side of an object, such as when holding a tumbler.

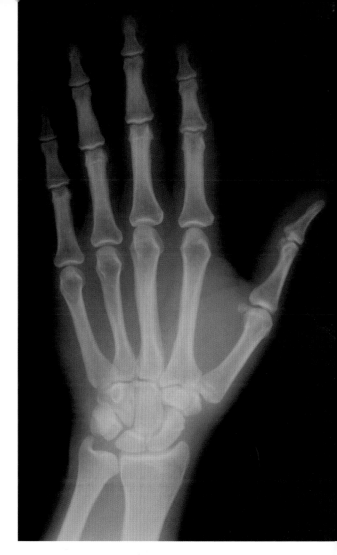

An X-ray of an adult human wrist and hand shows the carpal (wrist), metacarpal (palm) and phalanges (finger) bones.

ANIMAL VERSUS HUMAN

An orang-utan has very long fingers but a short thumb. It can only hold with a hook-like grip. It hangs from its hands as it swings through the trees.

The orang-utan's hook-like hand and small thumb.

Top Tips

Muscles that are used too much or too suddenly, get tired or fatigued. They become weak and begin to shake. In the hand, this makes delicate movements difficult. Practice usually helps, as does taking a break to relax, stretch and move the fingers in other directions.

THE SHOULDER AND ARM

A range of movements

There are only three bones in the arm – the humerus in the upper part, and the radius and ulna which lie alongside each other in the lower part or forearm. Yet the arm can reach up, forwards, down and even around the back. This is due mainly to the very wide range of motion at the shoulder joint, the more limited bending of the elbow, and also 'rotation'. This happens when bones twist or rotate. The wrist may seem very flexible because the hand can bend forwards and backwards, and also twist around almost in a circle. In fact, the twisting happens all along the arm (see panel).

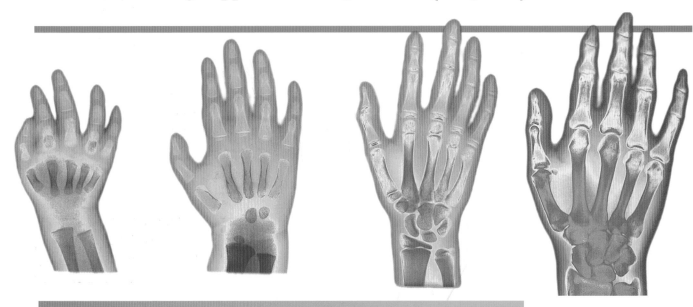

Try this!

Hold your arm out straight in front, palm up. Twist it so the palm turns to face down. Keep going and see how the hand can turn almost in a full circle, so the palm nearly faces upwards again. Now, do this while holding your forearm firmly, halfway along, with your other hand. The palm turns much less, because the only twisting motion is at the wrist. In the first case, the whole arm was involved, as its long bones twisted along their lengths.

This series of X-ray pictures shows a baby's hand growing into an adult hand. The skeleton in the wrist and hand forms first as cartilage and gradually hardens into bone, coloured blue. (See also page 37.)

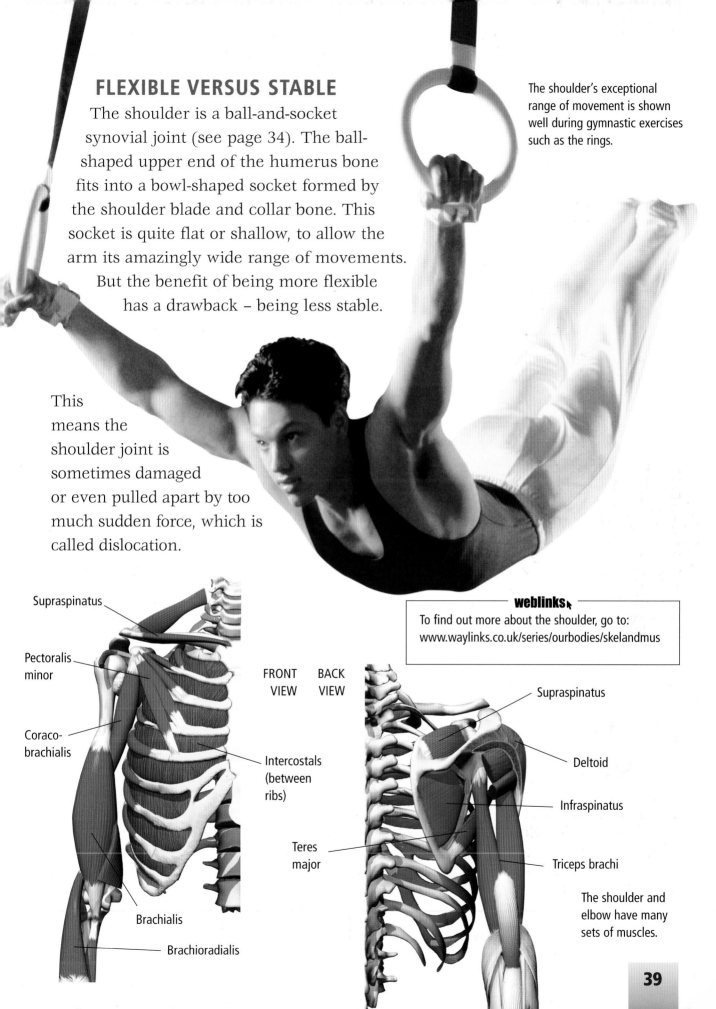

FLEXIBLE VERSUS STABLE

The shoulder is a ball-and-socket synovial joint (see page 34). The ball-shaped upper end of the humerus bone fits into a bowl-shaped socket formed by the shoulder blade and collar bone. This socket is quite flat or shallow, to allow the arm its amazingly wide range of movements. But the benefit of being more flexible has a drawback – being less stable.

The shoulder's exceptional range of movement is shown well during gymnastic exercises such as the rings.

This means the shoulder joint is sometimes damaged or even pulled apart by too much sudden force, which is called dislocation.

weblinks
To find out more about the shoulder, go to:
www.waylinks.co.uk/series/ourbodies/skelandmus

Supraspinatus

Pectoralis minor

Coraco-brachialis

FRONT VIEW   BACK VIEW

Intercostals (between ribs)

Brachialis

Brachioradialis

Teres major

Supraspinatus

Deltoid

Infraspinatus

Triceps brachi

The shoulder and elbow have many sets of muscles.

39

THE LEG AND FOOT

Differently designed

The leg and foot have almost the same number of bones and muscles as the arm and hand. But they are designed less for being flexible, and more for carrying the body's weight. The hip is a ball-and-socket synovial joint, like the shoulder. But the bowl-like socket is deeper than the socket in the shoulder. This means the leg has a smaller range of movements than the arm. However the hip joint is much stronger and more stable or secure, and less likely to dislocate (come apart).

The power of the leg muscles can propel the whole body more than two metres off the ground, as when high-jumping.

BIG AND UNUSUAL

The biggest single joint in the body is the knee. It is unusual in two ways. It has ligaments inside it, as well as around it. There are two inner ligaments between the bones, called the cruciate ligaments because they form a cross or X shape. The knee also has two extra cushion-like pieces of cartilage which 'float' in the joint, between the bone ends. These are crescent- or moon-shaped and called menisci. People such as football players and skiers who move quickly and then stop, and twist and turn at speed, put great strain on their knees. They may suffer 'cruciate trouble' or 'cartilage (meniscus) problems'. The hip and leg also have the body's largest muscle. This is the gluteus maximus, which forms part of the buttock. It pulls the thigh back as we jump and leap.

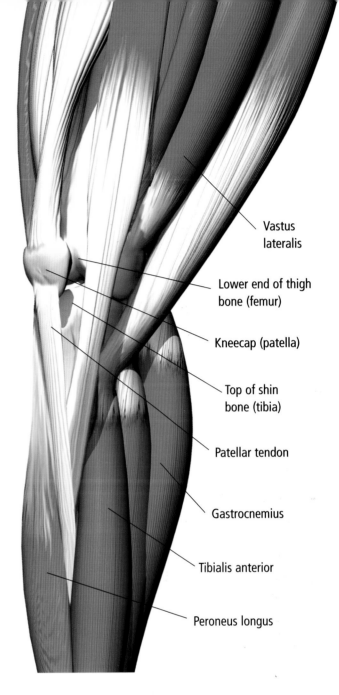

Vastus lateralis

Lower end of thigh bone (femur)

Kneecap (patella)

Top of shin bone (tibia)

Patellar tendon

Gastrocnemius

Tibialis anterior

Peroneus longus

Top Tips

Cramp is very painful tensing or contraction of a muscle, which feels hard and 'knotted'. Cramp tends to affect muscles which are used suddenly after long periods of inactivity. The remedy is to stretch the muscle gently by moving the body part, and massage it. However medical advice is needed for cramps that occur frequently or continue for long periods.

In the knee, the rounded knuckle-like lower end of the femur (thigh bone) fits into the slightly dished top of the tibia (shin bone). The kneecap or patella is an unusual bone because it is entirely inside a large tendon, called the patellar tendon. It protects the knee joint at the front.

BACK JOINTS AND MUSCLES

A tower of strength

The backbone or spine is the main 'girder' or 'tower' of the body, holding up the head, arms and torso (central body). It is not one bone, but a chain-like row of 26 bones known as vertebrae. There are seven vertebrae in the neck region, 12 in the chest (each one joined to a pair of ribs), five in the lower back, one in the hip region joined to the hip bones, and one small 'tail' bone at the lower end. A tunnel runs through the whole backbone. Inside it, well protected, is the body's main nerve – the spinal cord.

BACK MUSCLES

Each vertebra has long rod-like extensions called neural spines or processes. These are anchor points where muscles are attached. About 25 sets of long, slim muscles run up and down the backbone, overlapping each other. They join to different sets of vertebrae, and link the backbone to the head, shoulders, ribs and hips. These vertebral muscles give the whole backbone great strength. They also hold the shoulders and hips steady as the arms and legs move.

Sets of long back muscles hold the back upright when standing, and allow it to bend and twist. The cartilage pad or disc, between each pair of bones in the back, is very strong and tough. It has an outer layer made of stringy fibres, and a slightly more flexible inner layer, or centre, almost like stiff jelly.

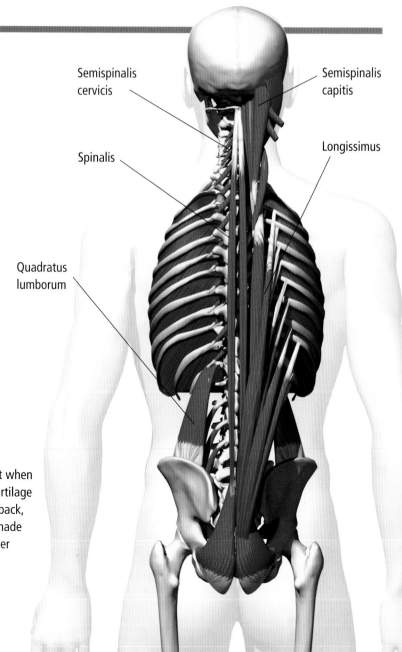

Semispinalis cervicis

Semispinalis capitis

Spinalis

Longissimus

Quadratus lumborum

JOINTS IN THE BACK

The vertebral bones have specialized joints. Each has a pad of cartilage between its two vertebrae, that works like a cushion to absorb knocks and jolts, and to let the bones move and tilt slightly. The pad is called the intervertebral disc (see page 34). The disc and the joint's structure allow the two bones to move only slightly in relation to each other. But along the whole backbone, these small movements add up, so the back can bend almost 'double' in a U shape.

Try this!

Stand up straight, then slowly and carefully, bend your back to the front, side and rearwards. (Do not strain it.) Which direction is easiest and most flexible? The joints between the vertebrae also allow twisting, so you can keep your feet still, but turn around so your head can look backwards.

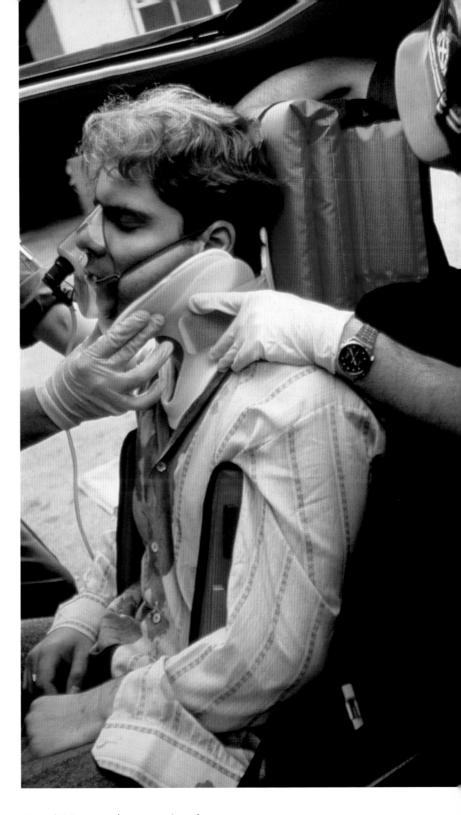

A neck injury may be very serious, because of the risk of damage to the spinal cord, which carries nerve signals between brain and body. A neck guard or stabilizer is carefully fitted to hold and support the head during transport to hospital or medical centre.

JOINT PROBLEMS

Back strain

Everyday actions such as walking, jogging and correct lifting rarely strain the joints. One exception is the back. A back strain is more likely if a person lifts a heavy load by leaning over and bending the back, and perhaps twisting as well, rather than by bending at the hips and knees. Sometimes one of the pads or discs between two backbones gets squeezed so much, it bulges at a weak point in its outer layer and presses on a nearby nerve, causing great pain. The bulge is called a prolapsed (or 'slipped') disc.

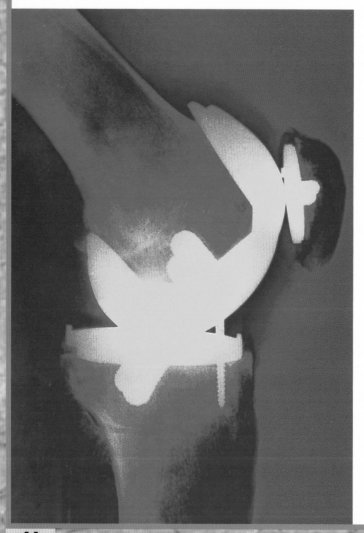

ARTHRITIS

The scientific name for a joint is an arthrosis. The main problems which affect joints, producing pain and swelling, are known as arthritis. There are several types. In osteoarthritis a joint becomes worn, and in particular, the smooth cartilage in the joint becomes rough and flaky. This is made more likely by old age, too much strain on the joints over the years, and previous injuries. The joints are stiff and aching, especially in the morning after a night's rest.

Many types of artificial joints, such as this knee, are based on the design of the real joint within the body, and allow a similar range of movements.

SELF-ATTACK

Rheumatoid arthritis is a complicated disease where the body's immune system, which is supposed to attack invading germs, mistakenly attacks parts of the body itself. This is known as an auto-immune problem. The attacked joints become swollen, painful, stiff and deformed with lumps. In younger people rheumatoid arthritis is more common compared to osteoarthritis, but it is still a rare condition.

TREATMENTS

Many kinds of medicinal drugs can help different forms of arthritis. So can an operation, either to treat the affected parts, or to replace them with an artificial joint made of special, hard-wearing plastic and metal.

HEALTHY MUSCLES AND BONES

The body's musculo-skeletal system is designed for movement and activity. But unsuitable activity and excessive strain can lead to problems – as can under-use of the system due to inactivity.

MICRO-BODY

The cartilage in a joint affected by osteoarthritis is rough, pitted and crumbly, rather than smooth and slightly bendy.

Experts such as sports coaches and exercise leaders can give advice about keeping the right balance.

weblinks

To find out more about joint problems, go to:
www.waylinks.co.uk/series/ourbodies/skelandmus

Swimming allows the body to be active while supported by water.

GLOSSARY

actin One of the two main substances shaped as long, thin filaments which, with myosin, is grouped in bundles to form a muscle fibril, and which slides past filaments of myosin to make a muscle contract.

antagonistic To work against or oppose, as in antagonistic muscle partners attached to one bone, which pull the bone in different or opposite ways.

bone marrow A soft, jelly-like substance in the middle of some bones.

calcium An important mineral for the body, which in crystal form gives strength and hardness to bones and teeth, and also keeps other parts of the body, such as nerves, healthy.

cancellous (spongy) bone A fairly strong but also lightweight, honeycomb-type of bone, which forms the middle layer of most bones.

cardiac muscle The type of muscle that forms the walls of the heart.

cartilage A strong, tough, lightweight, fairly stiff but slightly bendy substance, that makes up structural parts of the body such as inside the nose and ears, and which also covers the ends of bones in most types of joints.

cell A single unit or 'building block' of life – the human body is made of billions of cells of many different kinds.

collagen An important structural substance in the body – a protein made of many tiny, strong, tough fibres that occurs in the skin, tendons and many other parts of the body.

compact (hard) bone A strong, hard, dense type of bone, which forms the outer layer or 'shell' of most bones, around the less strong cancellous (spongy) layer.

contract In a muscle, when it tenses and pulls and becomes shorter.

hormones Natural body chemicals made by parts called endocrine glands, that circulate in blood and control many processes such as growth, the use of energy, water balance and the formation of urine.

involuntary muscles See visceral muscles.

ligament A strong, slightly stretchy, usually strap-shaped part, that holds two bones together at a joint to limit their movements and stop them coming apart.

marrow See bone marrow.

muscle fibres Long, thin, thread-shaped parts (myofibres) that are grouped in bundles to make up the bulk of a muscle.

muscle fibrils Long, thin, thread-shaped parts (myofibrils) that are grouped in bundles to make up the bulk of a muscle fibre.

myofibre See muscle fibres.

myofibril See muscle fibrils.

myosin One of the two main substances shaped as long, thin filaments which, with actin, is grouped in bundles to form a muscle fibril, and which slides past filaments of actin to make a muscle contract.

oxygen A gas making up one-fifth of air, which has no colour, taste or smell, but which is vital for breaking down nutrients inside the body to obtain energy for life processes.

peristalsis The wave-like, squeezing motion of muscles, especially where they form a tube or bag and squeeze to move along the contents.

FURTHER INFORMATION

phosphate A mineral made from the substances phosphorus and oxygen, which in crystal form gives strength and hardness to bones and teeth.

relax In a muscle, when it is no longer tense and pulling, but becomes floppy and can be pulled longer or stretched.

skeletal muscles Types of muscles which are mostly joined to the bones of the skeleton, and which are voluntary, able to be moved at will (rather than working automatically without conscious will), and which have tiny stripes or striations when seen under the microscope.

skeleton All of the body's bones and also the supporting parts made of cartilage, or 'gristle'.

smooth muscles See visceral muscles.

striped muscles See skeletal muscles.

tendon A very strong, tough, fibrous, rope-like part, where a muscle tapers thinner and anchors to a bone or to another muscle.

visceral muscles Types of muscles which are mostly deep within the body, especially in the chest and abdomen, but are not joined to the bones of the skeleton, and which are involuntary (working automatically without conscious will), and which look 'smooth' under the microscope because they lack tiny stripes or striations.

vitamins The naturally-occurring substances either made by the body or taken up in food, which are needed to keep the body healthy and avoid illness.

voluntary muscles See skeletal muscles.

BOOKS

Body Focus: Bones/Muscles (Heinemann, 2004)
Body Science: How We Move/The Human Skeleton (Frankin Watts, 2004)
Eyewitness Guides: Skeleton by Steve Parker (Dorling Kindersley, 2004)
Under the Microscope: Muscles/Skeleton (Franklin Watts, 2001)

ORGANIZATIONS

Muscular Dystrophy Campaign
A UK charity focusing on all muscular dystrophies and allied disorders, which has pioneered the search for treatments and cures for over 40 years and provides support to people affected by the condition.
7–11 Prescott Place, London SW4 6BS
Tel: 020 7720 8055

National Osteoporosis Society
The only national UK charity dedicated to improving the diagnosis, prevention and treatment of this fragile bone disease.
Camerton, Bath BA2 0PJ   Tel: 01761 471771

Arthritis Care
The UK's largest voluntary organization working with and for people with arthritis.
18 Stephenson Way, London NW1 2HD
Tel: 020 7380 6500

BackCare
Registered as National Back Pain Association (Charity No.256751)
The charity for healthier backs is dedicated to educating people on how to avoid preventable back pain, and supporting those living with back pain.
16 Elmtree Road, Teddington
Middlesex, TW11 8ST
Tel: 020 8977 5474

INDEX

CONTENTS

Guide to symbols

The recipes in this book are accompanied by symbols that alert you to important information.

 Tells you how many people the recipe serves, or how much is produced.

 Indicates how much time you will need to prepare and cook a dish. Next to this symbol you will also find out if additional time is required for such things as marinating, standing, proving, or cooling. You need to read the recipe to find out exactly how much extra time is needed.

 Alerts you to what has to be done before you can begin to cook the recipe, or to parts of the recipe that take a long time to complete.

 Denotes that special equipment is required. Where possible, alternatives are given.

 Accompanies freezing information.

Techniques

Make stock

A good stock is vital for a well-flavoured soup. Simply simmering a well-balanced combination of vegetables together produces a light, fragrant vegetable stock, or you can use bones to produce a gelatinous stock that is rich in flavour.

Chicken stock

1 Place either raw chicken bones, the whole carcass, or the bones and scraps from a cooked chicken in a large saucepan or stockpot with some aromatic vegetables and fresh herbs, and cover with water.

2 Bring to the boil, then reduce the heat and simmer for 2–3 hours, skimming off any foam that rises to the surface with a slotted spoon. Strain into a bowl through a fine sieve and leave to cool.

3 Once the stock has cooled, place it in the refrigerator. Any fat will congeal on the surface, and can then be removed with a slotted spoon.

Fish stock

1 Put some fish trimmings and heads (blood rinsed off, bones cracked, trimmings cut into even-sized pieces) in a large pan. Avoid using oily fish such as mackerel, which produce an unpleasant flavour.

2 Roughly chop some aromatic vegetables (onions, celery, and carrots all work well) and add them to the pot, along with some fresh herbs. Cover with water and bring to the boil over a high heat.

3 Once the stock reaches the boil, lower the heat, and simmer for 20 minutes (any longer and the stock will start to become bitter). Skim off the scum that rises to the surface with a slotted spoon.

4 Ladle the stock through a fine sieve into a bowl, pressing the solid ingredients against the sieve to extract as much liquid as possible. Allow to cool, then refrigerate.

Gazpacho

This chilled Spanish soup is always popular when the weather is hot.

INGREDIENTS

1 kg (2¼lb) tomatoes, plus extra
  to serve
1 small cucumber, peeled and finely
  chopped, plus extra to serve
1 small red pepper, deseeded and
  chopped, plus extra to serve
2 garlic cloves, crushed

4 tbsp sherry vinegar
salt and freshly ground black pepper
120ml (4fl oz) extra virgin olive oil, plus
  extra to serve
1 hard-boiled egg, white and yolk
  separated and chopped, to serve

METHOD

1 Bring a kettle of water to the boil. Place the tomatoes in a heatproof bowl, pour over enough boiling water to cover, and leave for 20 seconds, or until the skins split. Drain and cool under cold running water. Gently peel off the skins, cut the tomatoes in half, deseed, and chop the flesh.

2 Put the tomato flesh, cucumber, red pepper, garlic, and sherry vinegar in a food processor or blender. Season to taste with salt and pepper, and process until smooth. Pour in the olive oil and process again. Dilute with a little water if too thick. Transfer the soup to a serving bowl, cover with cling film, and chill for at least 1 hour.

3 When ready to serve, finely chop the extra cucumber and red pepper. Place the cucumber, pepper, and egg yolk and egg white in individual bowls and arrange on the table, along with a bottle of olive oil. Ladle the soup into bowls and serve, letting each diner add their own garnish.

serves 4

prep 15 mins,
plus chilling

chill for at
least 1 hr

food processor
or blender

freeze, without
the garnishes,
for up to 1 month

Watercress soup

Serve this velvety smooth soup hot,
topped with Parmesan cheese.

INGREDIENTS
25g (scant 1 oz) butter
1 onion, peeled and finely chopped
175g (6 oz) watercress
3 ripe pears, cored and roughly chopped
1 litre (1¾ pints) vegetable stock
salt and freshly ground black pepper
200ml (7fl oz) double cream
juice of ½ lemon
Parmesan cheese, grated, to serve
olive oil, to drizzle

METHOD
1 Melt the butter in a saucepan and cook the onion for 10 minutes, or until soft, stirring
occasionally to prevent burning.
2 Meanwhile, trim the watercress and pick off the leaves. Add the watercress stalks to the
onion with the pears and stock, and season with salt and pepper.
3 Bring to the boil, cover and simmer gently for 15 minutes. Remove from the heat and
pour into a blender along with the watercress leaves. Process until the soup has a very
smooth texture.
4 Stir in the cream and lemon juice, adjust the seasoning, and serve sprinkled with
Parmesan and drizzled with a little oil.

serves 4

prep 10 mins
• cook 15 mins

blender

freeze the soup, before
the cream is added, for
up to 3 months

Vichyssoise

Despite its French name, this silky, smooth iced soup originates from America and may also be served hot.

INGREDIENTS

30g (1 oz) butter

3 large leeks, green ends discarded, finely sliced

2 potatoes, about 175g (6 oz) in total, peeled and chopped

1 celery stick, roughly chopped

1.2 litres (2 pints) vegetable stock

salt and freshly ground black pepper

150ml (5fl oz) double cream, plus extra to serve

2 tbsp finely chopped chives, to serve

METHOD

1 Heat the butter in a heavy saucepan over a medium heat and add the leeks. Press a piece of damp greaseproof paper on top, cover, and cook, shaking gently from time to time, for 15 minutes, or until the leeks are softened and golden.

2 Add the potatoes, celery, and stock, and season with salt and pepper. Bring to the boil, stirring, then cover and simmer for 30 minutes, or until the vegetables are tender.

3 Remove the pan from the heat and leave to cool slightly, then process in a blender until very smooth, in batches if necessary. Season to taste with salt and pepper and allow the soup to cool completely before stirring in the cream. Chill for at least 3 hours before serving.

4 To serve, pour into serving bowls, lightly stir in a little extra cream, and sprinkle with chives and black pepper.

 serves 4

 prep 15 mins, plus chilling • cook 45 mins

 chill for at least 3 hrs

 blender

 freeze, before the cream is added, for up to 3 months

Tomato soup

Easy to make, this delicious soup can be
enjoyed all year round.

INGREDIENTS
1 tbsp olive oil
1 onion, chopped
1 garlic clove, sliced
2 celery sticks, sliced
1 carrot, sliced
1 potato, chopped
2 x 400g cans tomatoes
750ml (1¼ pints) vegetable stock or
  chicken stock
1 bay leaf
1 tsp sugar
salt and freshly ground black pepper

METHOD
1 Heat the oil in a large saucepan over a medium-low heat, add the onion, garlic, and
  celery, and fry, stirring frequently, until softened but not coloured.
2 Add the carrot and potato and stir for 1 minute, then add the tomatoes with their juice,
  stock, bay leaf, and sugar. Season to taste with salt and pepper, bring to the boil, then
  reduce the heat, cover, and simmer for 45 minutes, or until the vegetables are very soft.
3 Remove from the heat, discard the bay leaf, and allow to cool slightly, then process in a
  blender or food processor until smooth, working in batches if necessary. Taste and
  adjust the seasoning, then reheat and serve. Garnish with celery leaves and swirls of
  double cream, if you like.

serves 4

prep 20 mins
• cook 55 mins

blender or
food processor

Mushroom soup

Using a selection of both wild and cultivated mushrooms will produce a soup that is bursting with flavour.

INGREDIENTS
30g (1 oz) butter
1 onion, finely chopped
2 celery sticks, finely chopped
1 garlic clove, crushed
450g (1lb) mixed mushrooms, roughly
  chopped
200g (7 oz) potatoes, peeled and cubed
1 litre (1¾ pints) vegetable stock
2 tbsp finely chopped flat-leaf parsley
salt and freshly ground black pepper

METHOD
1 Melt the butter in a large saucepan, add the onion, celery, and garlic, and fry for 3–4 minutes, or until softened.
2 Stir in the mushrooms and continue to fry for a further 5–6 minutes. Add the potatoes and stock and bring up to the boil. Reduce the heat and leave to simmer gently for 30 minutes.
3 Use a hand blender to process the soup until smooth. Sprinkle in the parsley and season to taste with salt and pepper. Serve immediately.

serves 4

prep 10 mins
• cook 45 mins

hand blender

freeze for
up to 3 months

Carrot and orange soup

A light, refreshing soup with a hint of spice –
this is perfect for summer.

INGREDIENTS

2 tsp light olive oil or sunflower oil
1 leek, sliced
500g (1lb 2 oz) carrots, sliced
1 potato, about 115g (4 oz), chopped
½ tsp ground coriander
pinch of ground cumin
300ml (10fl oz) orange juice
500ml (16fl oz) vegetable stock or
  chicken stock
1 bay leaf
salt and freshly ground black pepper
2 tbsp chopped coriander, to garnish

METHOD

1 Place the oil, leek, and carrots in a large saucepan and cook over a low heat for
  5 minutes, stirring frequently, or until the leek has softened. Add the potato, coriander,
  and cumin, then pour in the orange juice and stock. Add the bay leaf and stir.
2 Increase the heat, bring the soup to the boil, then lower the heat, cover, and simmer for
  40 minutes, or until the vegetables are very tender.
3 Allow the soup to cool slightly, discard the bay leaf, then transfer to a blender or food
  processor and process until smooth, working in batches if necessary.
4 Return to the saucepan and add a little extra stock or water if the soup is too thick.
  Bring back to a simmer, then transfer to heated serving bowls and sprinkle with
  chopped coriander. Garnish with a drizzling of double cream, if you like.

serves 4

prep 10 mins
• cook 40 mins

blender or
food processor

Thick vegetable soup

This filling soup is a good winter warmer.

INGREDIENTS

2 tbsp olive oil
2 onions, finely chopped
salt and freshly ground black pepper
4 garlic cloves, grated or finely chopped
1 tbsp rosemary leaves, finely chopped
4 celery sticks, finely chopped
4 carrots, finely chopped
4 courgettes, finely chopped
2 x 400g cans whole tomatoes, chopped
  in the can
1.2 litres (2 pints) hot vegetable stock
handful of flat-leaf parsley, finely
  chopped

METHOD

1 Heat the oil in a large pan, add the onions, and cook over a low heat for 6–8 minutes, or until soft and translucent. Season with salt and black pepper, then add the garlic, rosemary, celery, and carrots and cook over a low heat, stirring occasionally, for 10 minutes.
2 Add the courgettes and cook for 5 minutes, then stir in the tomatoes, and squash with the back of a fork. Add the stock, bring to the boil, then reduce to a simmer and cook for 20 minutes. Season well with salt and pepper, then stir through the parsley. Serve with fresh crusty bread.

serves 8

prep 15 mins
• cook 45 mins

freeze for up
to 3 months

Fish soup with saffron & fennel

This rustic soup is simple to prepare and sure to please.

INGREDIENTS

30g (1 oz) butter

3 tbsp olive oil

1 large fennel bulb, finely chopped

2 garlic cloves, crushed

1 small leek, sliced

4 ripe plum tomatoes, chopped

3 tbsp brandy

¼ tsp saffron threads, soaked in
a little hot water

zest of ½ orange

1 bay leaf

1.7 litres (3 pints) fish stock

300g (10 oz) potatoes, diced and
parboiled for 5 minutes

4 tbsp dry white wine

500g (1lb 2oz) fresh black mussels,
scrubbed and debearded

salt and freshly ground black pepper

500g (1lb 2oz) monkfish or firm white
fish, cut into bite-sized pieces

6 raw whole tiger prawns

flat-leaf parsley, chopped, to serve

METHOD

1 Heat the butter with 2 tablespoons of the oil in a large, deep pan. Stir in the fennel, garlic, and leek, and fry over a moderate heat, stirring occasionally, for 5 minutes, or until softened and lightly browned.

2 Stir in the tomatoes, add the brandy, and boil rapidly for 2 minutes, or until the juices are reduced slightly. Stir in the saffron in its water, orange zest, bay leaf, fish stock, and potatoes. Bring to the boil, then reduce the heat and skim off any scum from the surface. Cover and simmer for 20 minutes, or until the potatoes are tender. Remove the bay leaf.

3 Meanwhile, heat the remaining oil with the wine in a large deep pan until boiling. Add the mussels, cover, and continue cooking on a high heat for 2–3 minutes, shaking the pan often. Discard any mussels that do not open. Strain, reserving the liquid, and set the mussels aside.

4 Add the liquid to the soup and season to taste with salt and pepper. Bring to the boil, add the monkfish pieces and prawns, then reduce the heat, cover, and simmer gently for 5 minutes, or until the fish is just cooked and the prawns are pink. Add the mussels to the pan and bring almost to the boil.

5 Serve the soup sprinkled with chopped parsley.

serves 4–6

prep 10 mins
• cook 1 hr

before cooking, tap the
mussels and discard
any that do not close

Tuscan bean soup

This classic dish, *Ribollita*, is named after the traditional method of re-boiling soup from the day before. The flavours will improve if made a day in advance.

INGREDIENTS

4 tbsp extra virgin olive oil, plus extra
　　for drizzling
1 onion, chopped
2 carrots, sliced
1 leek, sliced
2 garlic cloves, chopped
400g can chopped tomatoes
1 tbsp tomato purée
900ml (1½ pints) chicken stock

salt and freshly ground black pepper
400g can borlotti beans, flageolet
　　beans, or cannellini beans, drained
　　and rinsed
250g (9 oz) baby spinach leaves or
　　spring greens, shredded
8 slices ciabatta bread
grated Parmesan cheese, for sprinkling

METHOD

1　Heat the oil in a large saucepan and fry the onion, carrots, and leek over a low heat for 10 minutes, or until softened but not coloured. Add the garlic and fry for 1 minute. Add the tomatoes, tomato purée, and stock. Season to taste with salt and pepper.
2　Mash half the beans with a fork and add to the pan. Bring to the boil, then lower the heat and simmer for 30 minutes.
3　Add the remaining beans and spinach to the pan. Simmer for a further 30 minutes.
4　Toast the bread until golden and drizzle with olive oil. Spoon the soup into the bowls, top with a sprinkling of Parmesan, drizzle with a little more olive oil, and serve with the toast.

serves 4

prep 15 mins
• cook 1 hr
20 mins

Hungarian goulash soup

A traditional, warming soup flavoured with beef, onions, tomato, and paprika.

INGREDIENTS

120ml (4fl oz) olive oil
675g (1½ lb) onions, peeled and sliced
2 garlic cloves, crushed
675g (1½ lb) chuck steak, cut into
   5cm (2 in) cubes
salt and freshly ground black pepper
2 tbsp paprika

1 tsp caraway seeds
1 tsp cayenne pepper, plus extra, for
   sprinkling
4 tbsp tomato purée
1 litre (1¾ pints) beef stock
soured cream, to serve

METHOD

1 Heat a large flameproof casserole over medium heat with 3 tablespoons of the olive oil and cook the onions for 10 minutes, or until golden brown. Add the garlic for the final 2 minutes, stirring occasionally.

2 Meanwhile, in a separate pan, heat the remaining oil and brown the meat on all sides.

3 Season the meat with salt and add it to the onions, along with the spices and tomato purée. Cook for 5 minutes, stirring all the time, before adding the stock.

4 Simmer gently for 1 hour 45 minutes, or until the meat is very tender. Season to taste with salt and pepper, and serve with soured cream and a sprinkling of cayenne pepper.

serves 6–8

prep 15 mins
• cook 2 hrs

large flameproof
casserole

French onion soup

This Parisian classic is given extra punch
with spoonfuls of brandy.

INGREDIENTS

30g (1 oz) butter

1 tbsp sunflower oil

675g (1½ lb) onions, thinly sliced

1 tsp sugar

salt and freshly ground black pepper

120ml (4fl oz) red wine

2 tbsp plain white flour

1.5 litres (2¾ pints) beef stock

4 tbsp brandy

1 garlic clove, cut in half

4 slices of baguette, about 2cm (¾in)
   thick, toasted

115g (4 oz) Gruyère cheese or Emmental
   cheese, grated

METHOD

1 Melt the butter with the oil in a large, heavy pan over a low heat. Stir together the
   onions and sugar and season to taste with salt and pepper. Press a piece of wet,
   greaseproof paper over the surface and cook, stirring occasionally, uncovered, for
   40 minutes, or until the onions are rich and dark golden brown. Take care that they
   do not stick and burn on the bottom.

2 Remove the paper and stir in the wine. Increase the heat to medium and stir for
   5 minutes, or until the onions are glazed. Sprinkle with the flour and stir for 2 minutes.
   Stir in the stock and bring to the boil. Reduce the heat to low, cover, and leave the soup
   to simmer for 30 minutes. Taste and adjust the seasoning, if necessary.

3 Meanwhile, preheat the grill on its highest setting. Divide the soup between
   4 flameproof bowls and stir 1 tablespoon of brandy into each. Rub the garlic clove
   over the toast and place 1 slice in each bowl. Sprinkle with the cheese and grill for
   2–3 minutes, or until the cheese is bubbling and golden. Serve at once.

serves 4

prep 10 mins
• cook 1 hr
20 mins

flameproof
soup bowls

freeze the soup, without
the bread or cheese, for
up to 1 month

New England clam chowder

Americans often serve this traditional, creamy soup with small saltine crackers.

INGREDIENTS

36 live clams
1 tbsp oil
115g (4 oz) thick-cut rindless streaky
  bacon rashers, diced
1 onion, finely chopped
2 floury potatoes, such as King Edward,
  peeled and cut into 1cm (½in) cubes

2 tbsp plain white flour
600ml (1 pint) whole milk
salt and freshly ground black pepper
125ml (4½fl oz) single cream
2 tbsp finely chopped flat-leaf parsley

METHOD

1 Discard any open clams. Shuck the clams and reserve the juice, adding enough water to make 600ml (1 pint). Chop the clams.
2 Heat the oil in a large, heavy saucepan. Fry the bacon over a medium heat, stirring frequently, for 5 minutes, or until crisp. Remove the bacon from the pan with a slotted spoon, drain on kitchen paper and set aside.
3 Add the onion and potatoes to the pan and fry for 5 minutes, or until the onion has softened. Add the flour and cook, stirring for 2 minutes.
4 Stir in the clam juice and milk and season to taste with salt and pepper. Bring to the boil, cover the pan, reduce the heat, and leave to simmer for 20 minutes or until the potatoes are tender. Add the clams and simmer gently, uncovered, for 5 minutes.
5 Stir in the cream and heat through without boiling. Serve hot, sprinkled with the bacon and parsley.

serves 4

prep 15 mins
• cook 35 mins

before cooking, tap the clams and discard any that do not close

Bouillabaisse

INGREDIENTS

4 tbsp olive oil
1 onion, thinly sliced
2 leeks, thinly sliced
1 small fennel bulb, thinly sliced
2–3 garlic cloves, finely chopped
4 tomatoes, skinned, deseeded,
  and chopped
1 tbsp tomato purée
250ml (9fl oz) dry white wine
1.5 litres (2¾ pints) fish stock
  or chicken stock
pinch of saffron threads
strip of orange zest
1 bouquet garni
salt and freshly ground black pepper

1.35kg (3lb) mixed white and oily fish and
  shellfish, such as gurnard, John Dory,
  monkfish, red mullet, prawns, and
  mussels, heads and bones removed
2 tbsp Pernod
8 thin slices day-old French bread,
  toasted, to serve

For the rouille

125g (4½ oz) mayonnaise
1 bird's-eye chilli, deseeded and roughly
  chopped
4 garlic cloves, roughly chopped
1 tbsp tomato purée
½ tsp salt

METHOD

1 Heat the oil in a large saucepan over a medium heat. Add the onion, leeks, fennel, and
  garlic and fry, stirring frequently, for 5–8 minutes, or until the vegetables are softened
  but not coloured. Add the tomatoes, tomato purée, and wine and stir until blended.
2 Add the stock, saffron, orange zest, and bouquet garni. Season to taste with salt and
  pepper, and bring to the boil. Reduce the heat, partially cover the pan, and simmer for
  30 minutes, or until the soup is reduced slightly, stirring occasionally.
3 To make the rouille, place all ingredients into a blender or food processor and process
  until smooth. Transfer to a bowl, cover with cling film, and chill until required.
4 Just before the liquid finishes simmering, cut the fish into chunks. Remove the orange
  zest and bouquet garni from the soup and add the firm fish. Reduce the heat to low and
  let the soup simmer for 5 minutes, then add the delicate fish and simmer for a further
  2–3 minutes, or until all the fish is cooked through and flakes easily. Stir in the Pernod,
  and season to taste with salt and pepper.
5 To serve, spread each piece of toast with rouille and put 2 slices in the bottom of each
  bowl. Ladle the soup on top and serve.

serves 4

prep 20 mins
• cook 45 mins

before cooking, tap the
mussels and discard
any that do not close

blender or
food processor

Chicken noodle soup

This spicy Mexican soup, *Sopa Seca de Fideos*, is made with thin fideo noodles, which are similar to angel hair pasta.

INGREDIENTS

2 large ripe tomatoes, skinned and deseeded

2 garlic cloves

1 small onion, roughly chopped

2 dried chipotle chillies, soaked

900ml (1½ pints) chicken stock

3 tbsp vegetable oil

2 skinless boneless chicken breasts, diced

225g (8 oz) Mexican fideo or dried angel hair pasta

4 tbsp soured cream, to serve

1 avocado, stone removed and chopped, to serve

METHOD

1 Put the tomatoes, garlic, onion, chillies, and 2 tablespoons of stock into a food processor or blender, and process to a purée. Set aside.

2 Heat 2 tablespoons of oil in a large pan and stir-fry the chicken for 2–3 minutes, or until just cooked. Remove from the pan, drain on kitchen paper, and set aside.

3 Add the remaining oil to the pan, add the noodles, and cook over a low heat until the noodles are golden, stirring constantly.

4 Pour in the tomato mixture, stir until the noodles are coated, then add the stock, and return the chicken to the pan. Cook the noodles for 2–3 minutes, or until just tender.

5 To serve, ladle into soup bowls, and top each with soured cream and chopped avocado.

serves 4

prep 20 mins
• cook 15 mins

soak the dried chillies in water for 30 mins before using

food processor or blender

Sweetcorn chowder

Full of potatoes and sweetcorn, this is a simple but tasty, chunky soup.

INGREDIENTS

2 tbsp olive oil
2 onions, finely chopped
salt and freshly ground black pepper
6–8 medium potatoes, cut into
  bite-sized pieces
2 x 340g cans sweetcorn, drained
1.4 litres (2½ pints) hot vegetable stock
handful of flat-leaf parsley, finely
  chopped
4 tbsp double cream (optional), to serve

METHOD

1 Heat the oil in a large pan, add the onions, and cook over a low heat for 6–8 minutes, or until soft and translucent. Season well with salt and black pepper, then stir in the potatoes and cook over a low heat for 5 minutes.
2 Mash the sweetcorn a little with the back of a fork, then add to the pan. Pour in the stock, bring to the boil, then reduce to a simmer and cook for 15 minutes, or until the potatoes are soft. Stir through the parsley and season again with salt and pepper if needed.
3 Stir through the cream (if using), ladle into bowls, and serve with fresh crusty bread.

serves 8   prep 15 mins   freeze for up to
              • cook 25 mins   3 months

Pea and mint soup

This no-cook soup preserves the fresh taste of its ingredients.

INGREDIENTS

250g (9 oz) frozen peas, such as
    petit pois
450ml (15fl oz) hot vegetable stock
handful of mint leaves, roughly chopped
a few thyme stalks, leaves picked
salt and freshly ground black pepper
1–2 tbsp crème fraîche (optional)
pinch of freshly grated nutmeg

METHOD

1 Put the peas in a bowl, pour over boiling water, and leave to stand for about
   5 minutes. Drain.
2 Using a blender, whiz the peas, stock, and herbs until smooth and combined.
   You may have to do this in batches. Add more stock if the soup is too thick. Season
   well with salt and pepper, and whiz again.
3 To serve, stir through the crème fraîche (if using), and top with a pinch of nutmeg. Serve
   hot or cold with crusty bread.

serves 4

prep 10 mins

blender

Mussels in fennel broth

This fragrant broth with coconut and juicy mussels makes an impressive dish.

INGREDIENTS

1 tbsp olive oil
1 onion, finely chopped
1 fennel bulb, trimmed and finely
   chopped
salt and freshly ground black pepper
2 garlic cloves, grated or finely chopped
2 waxy potatoes, peeled and finely diced
300ml (10fl oz) hot vegetable stock or
   light fish stock
400g can coconut milk
1.35kg (3lb) fresh mussels, scrubbed
   and debearded
handful of basil leaves, torn

METHOD

1 Heat the oil in a large pan over a low heat. Add the onion, fennel, and a pinch of salt, then sweat for about 5 minutes until softened. Add the garlic and potatoes, and cook for a few minutes more, being careful not to allow it to brown at all.

2 Pour in the stock, and bring to the boil. Add the coconut milk, reduce the heat slightly, and simmer gently for about 10 minutes, or until the potatoes are cooked. Bring back to the boil, add the mussels, and put a lid on the pan. Cook for about 5 minutes, until all the mussels are open (discard any that do not).

3 To serve, stir through the basil, taste the broth, and season if needed. Serve immediately.

serves 4

prep 10 mins
• cook 20 mins

before cooking, tap the
mussels and discard
any that do not close

Black bean and coconut soup

Caribbean flavours make this soup a great way to start a spicy main course.

INGREDIENTS

2 tbsp olive oil

2 red onions, finely chopped

2 bay leaves

salt and freshly ground black pepper

4 garlic cloves, grated or finely chopped

2 tsp ground cumin

2 tsp ground coriander

1 tsp chilli powder

2 x 400g cans black beans, drained and rinsed

1.2 litres (2 pints) hot vegetable stock

400ml can coconut milk

flour tortillas, to serve

METHOD

1 Heat the oil in a large pan, add the onions and bay leaves, and cook over a low heat for 6–8 minutes, or until the onions are soft and translucent. Season well with salt and pepper. Stir through the garlic, cumin, coriander, and chilli powder and cook for a few seconds.

2 Stir through the black beans, then pour in the stock and coconut milk. Bring to the boil, then reduce to a simmer and cook for 15–20 minutes. Remove the bay leaves and discard, then transfer the rest of the soup to a blender or food processor and pulse a couple of times so some of the beans are puréed and some remain whole. Add a little more hot stock if it is too thick. Season again with salt and pepper. Serve with tortilla triangles.

serves 8

prep 15 mins
• cook 30 mins

blender or
food processor

freeze for up to
3 months

Potato and leek soup

A simple soup using ingredients available year-round.

INGREDIENTS

450g (1lb) floury potatoes, peeled
1 tbsp olive oil
1 onion, finely chopped
4 leeks, cleaned and sliced
salt and freshly ground black pepper
900ml (1½ pints) hot vegetable stock
small handful of thyme leaves

METHOD

1 Boil the potatoes in a pan of salted water for 15–20 minutes until soft. Drain, then cut into bite-sized pieces.
2 Heat the olive oil in a large pan over a low heat. Add the onion, and sweat gently for about 5 minutes until soft and translucent. Add the leeks, and cook for a further 5 minutes. Season well with salt and pepper. Pour in the hot vegetable stock, and bring to the boil. Reduce the heat slightly, and simmer for about 10 minutes. Add the potatoes, and sprinkle in the thyme leaves. Continue cooking the soup until the potatoes are heated through, then serve hot with some fresh crusty bread.

serves 4

prep 5 mins
• cook 40 mins

Spiced butternut squash soup

You could use any winter squash for this spicy, comforting soup.

INGREDIENTS

2 tbsp olive oil
2 onions, finely chopped
salt and freshly ground black pepper
3 garlic cloves, grated or finely chopped
4 sage leaves, finely chopped
2 red chillies, deseeded and finely chopped
pinch of freshly grated nutmeg

1 large butternut squash or 2 small ones, halved, peeled, deseeded, and chopped into small pieces
2 potatoes, peeled and diced
1.4 litres (2½ pints) hot vegetable stock
chilli oil, to serve
grated Gruyère cheese, to serve

METHOD

1 Heat the oil in a large pan, add the onions, and cook over a low heat for 6–8 minutes, or until soft and translucent. Season with salt and black pepper, then stir through the garlic, sage, chillies, and nutmeg, and cook for a few seconds.
2 Stir in the squash, add the potatoes and stock, and bring to the boil. Reduce to a simmer and cook for 20–30 minutes, or until the squash and potatoes are soft. Transfer to a blender or food processor and whiz until smooth. Taste, and season again with salt and pepper. Serve with a drizzle of chilli oil, and a sprinkling of Gruyère cheese.

serves 8

prep 20 mins
• cook 40 mins

blender or food processor

freeze for up to 3 months

Split pea and bacon soup

This thick soup is a pleasure to eat. The bacon adds flavour, but can be left out for vegetarians.

INGREDIENTS

2 tbsp olive oil

425g (15 oz) bacon or pancetta, chopped into bite-sized pieces

2 onions, finely chopped

salt and freshly ground black pepper

4 celery sticks, finely chopped

4 carrots, finely chopped

550g (1¼lb) yellow split peas

1.7 litres (3 pints) hot vegetable stock

METHOD

1 Heat half the oil in a large heavy-based pan, add the bacon or pancetta, and cook over a medium heat, stirring occasionally, for 5 minutes, or until crispy and golden. Remove with a slotted spoon and put to one side. Heat the remaining oil in the pan, add the onions, and cook over a low heat for 6–8 minutes, or until soft and translucent. Season with salt and pepper, then add the celery and carrots and cook on a low heat for 5 minutes.

2 Add the peas and stock and bring to the boil slowly. Cover with a lid, reduce to a simmer, and cook for 2 hours, or until the peas are tender. Check occasionally, and top up with hot water if the soup begins to look too thick. Transfer to a blender or food processor and whiz until smooth and blended. Return to the pan with the bacon or pancetta, then season with salt and pepper to taste. Serve with fresh crusty bread.

serves 8

prep 15 mins • cook 2 hrs 20 mins

blender or food processor

freeze for up to 3 months

Senior Editor Cécile Landau

Designer Elma Aquino

Jacket Designer Mark Penfound

Special Sales Creative Project Manager Alison Donovan

Pre-Production Producer Rob Dunn

Producer Igrain Roberts

DK INDIA

Editorial Consultant Dipali Singh

Designer Neha Ahuja

DTP Designer Tarun Sharma

DTP Coordinator Sunil Sharma

Head of Publishing Aparna Sharma

This paperback edition published in 2017
First published in Great Britain in 2013
Material previously published in
The Cooking Book (2008) and *Cook Express* (2009)
by Dorling Kindersley Limited , 80 Strand, London WC2R 0RL

A CIP catalogue record for this book is available
from the British Library.

ISBN 978-0-2413-1817-1

Printed and bound in China

A WORLD OF IDEAS
SEE ALL THERE IS TO KNOW

www.dk.com